Population:

ONE

Discover Disability Changed
Into Extraordinary Ability

AVIVA
PUBLISHING
New York

Tyler McNamer

Population One:
Autism, Adversity, and the Will to Succeed

Address all inquiries to:
www.PopulationOne.com

Published by:
Aviva Publishing
Lake Placid, NY
518-523-1320
www.avivapubs.com

ISBN: 978-1-938686-54-2

Library of Congress Control Number: 2013XXXXXX

Edited by: Tyler Tichelaar

Cover & Interior Design: Fusion Creative Works,
www.fusioncw.com

Printed in the United States of America

First Edition

For additional copies, please visit: www.PopulationOne.com

DEDICATION

I dedicate this book to all those who are different, unique, and terrific. Just imagine if we were all the same? It really wouldn't be very fun, would it? I also want to dedicate this to all of the parents and teachers of the world. They bring an awesome impact on kids all around. This book is also dedicated to the children of the world. They are the best they can be, no matter what anyone says. Finally, I want to dedicate this book to my dear friends and "fans" and my loving family. They have played a huge part in my life, and I thank them.

ACKNOWLEDGMENTS

There are so many people I want to thank.

Kristina Tindall (Mom): For supporting me on this book and reminding me to have fun with this experience. For being my mom.

Jody McNamer (Dad): For inspiring me to be the best guy I can be. For being my dad.

Inga Tindall: For being my Mormor (Grandma). You brought a big impact to my life since I was a baby. Thank you for being my Mormor and making those delicious Swedish Pancakes.

Carmen McNamer: For being there for me when others were not. For helping me through my teen years, and always supporting me.

Teachers and Coaches: There are countless coaches and teachers whom I want to thank. They have taught me a lot from school lessons to how to get along with others. They are the ones who have done their job well helping me throughout my childhood.

John Whitehead: For being with me and teaching me things about my parents as I expressed in Chapter 12. For being one of my coaches.

Patrick Snow: For teaching me about books and how to do the whole publishing gig.

Tyler Tichelaar: For being my awesome editor! Thank you for making this book sound better. Well, better in grammar and spelling and all that stuff, but thank you for helping me edit this book.

Shiloh Schroeder: You helped me with the cover of this book, and I love it! Thank you very much.

I would like to give a special thanks to my Sponsors:

Platnum
Carmen McNamer

Gold
The Huey Family
Fred Rea
JJ Pawlowski

Silver
Steve McNamer

Bronze
Jerry Desmul
Jamie Penrod
Delinda Jokela
Brian Walker
Myra Walker
Chris Petersen
Carrie M. Cone
Brenne Schario
David Brimhall
Wendi Weith
Andre Martinez
Jennifer Smyth
Gina Zahajko

CONTENTS

INTRODUCTION

Being different from the masses is one of the greatest gifts that you possess! Let's face it: Who wants to be just like everyone else? Talk about boring! People come in all shapes and sizes and are born with natural and un-natural gifts and talents like no other, and your greatest challenge is to discover your gifts and then apply them to the world to create a better place, a better planet, a better universe! That is my challenge to you so that all of us can get along peacefully and become truly a population of one. As we begin, I would like to ask you some questions to help you discover what makes you unique, different, and awesome.

Are you different? Are you unique? Do you look different than others? Talk differently than others? Do you walk differently than others? Have you been born with talents that very few others have? Have you been brainwashed to look at your talents as a disability? Do you stay up nights dwelling on all the things in life you don't have, rather than focus on all the blessings you do have? Have you ever been bullied at school, at home, and in many areas in your life? Have you ever been called a "retard," "dumb," "disabled"? If you have answered "yes" to any of these questions, perhaps you have yet to understand, accept, and apply your unique gifts to make the world a better place.

If you have answered "Yes" to any of these questions, I feel your pain, I have walked in your shoes, and I can empathize with your situation. I have been bullied, called a retard, told that I am disabled, put in special classes, advised that I should not expect to reach my goals.

My name is Tyler McNamer and I have been called ALL of the above many, many times in my life. I am nineteen years old and have been blessed with autism my entire life. I have chosen to accept my label of autism not as a "disability" but as an "extraordinary ability" and I want to help you overcome the label that you may have suffered from for many years of your life.

So what is autism? The dictionary defines autism as a mental condition, present from early childhood, characterized by great difficulty in communicating and forming relationships with others. Also, it is defined as a mental condition in which fantasy dominates over reality.

So just how many people today are affected by this condition? According to a recent WebMD study, 1 in 88 kids today has autism and for boys the numbers is 1 in 54. Also you might be surprised to learn that since 2002, autism has increased by 78 percent. Let's put those numbers in perspective. A high school with 1,000 students enrolled is going to have 11-12 students with this condition, and a bigger high school with 2,500 students is going to have 28-29 students with autism.

So, now that you know more about autism, let me highlight some of the things you will learn by reading this book since I want to assure you that this book is not just a book about autism—it is a book about how we can all live together in harmony regardless of our differences. In this book, you are going to learn that, despite our differences and diversities, we can get along and become a population of one to serve others. In this book, you will learn the importance of becoming the leader in your own life, following your dreams. You will learn to focus on your blessings instead of being discouraged by your challenges. In this book, you will learn to embrace change and continue to learn for a lifetime. In this book, you will learn what it is like to be blessed with the unique ability of having autism. You will learn how not only to cope with your gifts, but to thrive in life and pursue your goals despite your challenges. In this book, you will learn how to turn your ability into a blessing to serve others and to be a mentor for others in need. In this book, you will learn how to create balance in your life; you will find out why, especially for me having autism, balance is so important and learn how many unbalanced people can gain control of their lives. Most importantly, you will learn how we can all co-exist together in harmony as a population of one to make our existence together better, more peaceful, more fulfilling and purposeful.

This book has fifty short chapters in it. You will find chapters on *Leadership, Change, Teamwork, Bullying, Embracing Change, Accepting Diversity, Balancing Your Life,* and many other subject matters that are important to this world. These subjects are all ones I speak on at schools and organizations all over the country. Additionally, in this book I have included many other chapters that may or may not be relevant to you and your journey. I have purposely included these chapters so you can get an inside look into my mind. I purposely want you to know, to understand, to learn how I (and perhaps many others who are gifted with the unique ability of autism) think. I want to give you a front row seat to my life, my mind, my special way of looking at the world. In some of the chapters, you will find information and ideas that you can apply to your life, while other chapters will simply allow you to understand me better.

Also, I have purposely requested that my editor keep my book in "my voice," and he assured me that he would do so and that this book will be grammatically correct, but he would also leave my writing the way that it is. It is "cool" and "different" and "unique" and perhaps you have never read a book such as this, but I promise you that some of what you read may inspire you to take action in your life, and other chapters that you read may just better help you understand my unique abilities. Regardless of which chapters you enjoy most, you will see firsthand how I (and tens of thousands of others) with the unique gift of autism think differently.

Additionally as a bonus in this book, you will read some chapters that have a "fantasy component" to them, which will bring you even more into my mind and the minds of others with autism. Therefore, if your life is boring and lacking some imagination, I think you will particularly enjoy these chapters.

Why me and why should you read this book? Well, first of all, having my unique ability of autism, I have graduated from high school, and I had the willingness to write a book at a young age for people with or without autism, young and old, and now I am pursuing my degree in college. I have been called a retard. I have been bullied. I have been a victim of others' limiting beliefs about my abilities, and yet, I have become the victor in my life and can help you do the same. I have become stronger because of the personal attacks, and more confident in my life as others have placed limitations on me. As a result, I am dedicating my life to serving and inspiring others who are different so they also can achieve their goals and blossom into the people they are true capable of becoming.

Most importantly, I am in the process of achieving my goals. I am an author and a professional speaker. I am a life coach, career coach, and a "unique abilities" coach who can help you along your journey to live your passions and spread a vision of peace and harmony throughout this universe.

However, I understand if you have apprehensions about pursuing your passions if you too share a unique ability. It is a difficult journey, and there will be many setbacks and obstacles along the way. It is hard to put yourself out there for others in the world to ridicule. There will be naysayers who will try to convince you to accept less and not pursue your life's biggest passions. There will be non-believers who will ridicule you for your differences. Your challenge will be to turn their disbeliefs in your abilities into extra fuel to be added to your fire and your driving force to succeed and achieve your goals.

Let's face it; if I can overcome all the challenges that have come into my life both in my past and in my future, then I can help you do the same. Therefore, I want to be the speaker for your school to help create an end to bullying. I want to be your mentor, your coach, and your example that despite the "unique gifts" and "differences" that you possess, you can indeed make a difference in this world and join me on my mission to help all humanity co-exist together as a population of one.

If I can do it, so can you! I believe in you! I want to help you! Are you ready to begin? Are you ready to lock arms with me and make this journey together? Are you ready to be the change you wish to see? Are you ready to change your life forever and impact the world like few others can? Are you ready to transform your differences into your best assets? If so, then let's make this journey together. Let's get started right now! Let's begin....

Your friend,

Tyler

FOREWORD

There was a time when the world was different. There is also a time when the world is different. And sometimes it takes a certain person to recognize those differences between generations, between the past and present, and why different generations came into existence before the world forgets them and moves on without the colorful generations of the past. I, Tyler McNamer, am that individual. Knowing that I have autism, I add on to my life and never erase the past. Anyone can write about anything, but what people can't do successfully is write about other people. It takes only one person to write about himself or herself. I'm proud to be one of those people. With this book, I will show you a different way of viewing the world through my eyes. Many people ask me why I am writing this book. I respond by saying, "Because it takes one mysterious person out of the darkness to inspire the world." That's how famous people got their fame. I have never thought of myself as famous; I'm just another person. I have never thought of myself as autistic, just highly unique... and a pretty awesome cool dude.

ABOUT THIS BOOK, BEING DIFFERENT, AND BEING A HERO

Different. That word alone is extremely common in everyday life. Especially when it comes to living beings. The way I used to see the word "different" was that it's a lonely thing, and because I am different, because I have autism, I felt like I didn't need anybody and needed to isolate myself from everyone.

Overall, because I was different I felt as if the planet needed me as a hero. That's what I thought before writing this book. In reality, I can't self-proclaim myself a hero. I'm just an individual. Are you an individual? If you are, then you are never alone. There are great people in the world we live in. People are great when they do good to themselves and to others. That is why, with this book, I want to prove that being an individual with or without autism can affect the world in a positive way.

All these years of being alone with freedom, I discovered something I wrote as a quote for my high school graduation: "The best kind of freedom is the freedom to do good. It's what makes heroes." I kept that quote as a reminder that doing good makes me feel like a hero to anyone and to anything. When I was little, I felt like a hero giving flowers to girls. It felt great. When creating this book, I felt like a brave hero because I was open to the thoughts coming from my heart and mind when writing and had the courage to help people young and old.

So many people in the world can write about anything, but only one person can write a book about me, and that is me. This is an autobiography about my childhood and how I viewed the world and what challenges I've faced over the years. Maybe most of you can relate to me when it comes to childhood stuff.

This book is not in an orderly fashion in terms of its chapters. I wrote what came up in my head. Most of the people I know are not named in this book.

This book can be described as many things. It can be a journal, a diary (not really), a survival kit, and a guide for everyone with or without autism. It can even be a comic book, but I can't draw comics. Although they look so cool! See, that's the thing about books and stories, there's a lot of imagination that's realistic most of the time.

With my help, I hope you can show great leadership, determination, and ambition. My book will give you examples of how to do that. Feel free to use my examples. If not, that's totally cool, because everyone is different and entitled to the choices he or she makes in life.

Enjoy the book.

1

WELCOME TO MY WORLD

There are many people named Tyler, but to tell the difference between people with the same name, I announce my full name almost everywhere I go. Since you are reading this, you can just call me Tyler. Throughout the years, with every step I take, I find my life quite entertaining. It's not entertaining in the way of saying, "It's fun all the time" because no one has ever had a completely fun life. Everyone makes mistakes; everyone puts forth effort to make his or her life great. Then later, it gets better depending on the person.

Let me tell you something personal about myself...well, I'll do much of that throughout this book, but I love to run—running makes me feel free. I run to school, I run to the store, I even use parkour training skills to run through obstacles just for fun. But I never run with anyone who's around me; the public I should say. Whenever I'm free and alone, running really gives me the strength to remember what was in the past, and it makes me think also about the present while using all that energy. Most of the time, my past has had memories that cannot be repeated. I have always wanted to relive them, but I can't do that. They are part of the past. Reliving them in my thoughts makes me feel so many emotions going on in my head that, sometimes, I even forget what is going on in the present.

My parents told me that writing calms me down whenever there is something crazy going on. It helps me express what I think. I bet you want to know why I'm writing a book and not a journal. A book of expressions and emotions tells even the writer what happened in his past. Journals are for people in the present so they can look back on their pasts, but they don't show their journals to the public.

A lot of things are meant to be secret, but for me, I don't believe that much in secrets. I view secrets as information people don't want to give out because they are not ready to say them yet. In this book, I will tell you what I see or what I saw in this world, and the secrets that will be revealed to my loved ones and to the acquaintances that want to understand my ways of viewing the world.

My book's title, *Population: One*, is very different from the titles of other books, as it should be. This very first chapter you're reading will tell you why I chose that title in the first place. I resemble everyone because like you, I am a world in myself.

You see, my friend, I have a world. You have a world. It represents who you are, what you are interested in, and what you like. I like the color red, so I have a red world. My favorite music is...well, I have a lot of favorites, but let's say jazz, my national music is jazz. What is your world like? Describe to me your character according to favorites, and you can make it into your own little world.

Color: _____

Music: _____

Food: _____

People: _____

Activity: _____

Game: _____

These are examples of a person's likes. With the "People" part of this, you can have statues of people you like, just like I have a statue of Chris Farley and of Elvis Presley. With the "Activity" and "Game" part, let's say Cricket can be your national pastime just like Baseball is America's favorite pastime, or is it American Football? Either or.

We have our own worlds in the galaxy. If there were another galaxy with life forms we never met before, they would be just like us. They would have their own worlds. The galaxies would come together for the universe. So let's recap.

Worlds = People

Galaxy = Planet Earth

Universe = Galaxy

? = Universe

Now why did I put a question mark next to the universe? Because no one can expand the universe except for the universe itself. There is no such thing as a second universe, unless if it's in video games or fictional books.

Population: One. It sounds like a lonely place, doesn't it? Well, it's not that bad when you can add more people to your world, and your population grows. How is that possible? I'll tell you.

When worlds collide, one of the worlds becomes human and lands on the other world. Take for example a party: You're invited to another person's world, and everyone's having a great time in that area. Then you leave the area, and become your own world once again. I've heard the saying "He/she is a part of my world" and that sort of gave me the idea about what my definition of a world really means.

Now, when worlds are by themselves, and they pass each other, the worlds react in a different way in their orbits. It's like saying flowers react to rain and sun by their growth. Everything reacts to something, just like when fire turns dark red when it's in contact with lithium chloride.

For a long time, I felt that my world effects other worlds in a negative way, and that's why my world was far away from the galaxy. It felt like that at first, until I looked even closer at space. There may be one person in a world, but even that person—male or female—can affect the galaxy and the universe in a way that's positive. There are people who are taller or smaller than you; then, there are people who have a lower IQ. But not me—because mine's higher. I'm joking; there are so many people who have different numbers for the intellectual mind. But those kinds of people can always come together as a "world" and soon become a galaxy, and all of that becomes the universe...as one.

2

EARLIEST MEMORY

When I was eleven months old, I was in an airplane. We were going to Sweden since that's where my great uncles and aunts live. My grandmother is Swedish and her name is Inga Tindall. Most of the time, I call her "Mormor," which is Swedish for "mother's mother." Kinda easy to say for babies I think. While I was in the plane, I looked outside and saw a giant iceberg just standing there as we flew over it. I stared at it for a long time; I thought it was amazing for me to see something over an ocean. I then saw the ocean and saw white sparkling water just as white as the iceberg. I literally thought that the iceberg made the ocean and it was what made the ocean cold and made it shine with the sparkling white color. When I came to Sweden, I saw a cup of water filled with ice. It reminded me of the iceberg I saw earlier. Sometime later, the ice melted. I was so sad, and I cried for a long time. Of course, I couldn't communicate back then or speak, so I later calmed down and went on with the vacation.

I went on a horseback ride on Great-Uncle Bo's horse. Riding on that horse made me feel like I was a good friend to the horse. I thought the horse was a big, tall, beautiful looking animal that could never do anything to hurt anyone. Later on in life, I learned that's not the case with any animal. They can all hurt people. A painted Swedish horse is a symbol of Sweden to me because when I look at green hills, strawberries, or horses, it feels like Sweden to me. When I think of the Swedish horse, I think of Sweden.

By the Baltic Sea, I was terrified by the water; after all, I thought icebergs made all water cold. I was proved wrong with the Baltic Sea. It wasn't as cold as I thought it would be. I used to spend so much time playing in the water, getting wet, and letting the water run through my hands. It was a great moment for me when I was eleven months old to experience water for the first time. I once drank some of the sea water, but then I learned that only kitchen water doesn't make you sick.

As I went back home to Portland, I saw that iceberg again; it was still standing there, and that iceberg now reminds me of my trip to Sweden; it was a great vacation. I hope that someday I will return to Sweden and to the other countries in Europe.

3

COMMUNICATION

As the years went by, I came to observe that everyone can talk. I was really sad that everyone gets to speak in words with their voices and communicate to each other. I could not say that to my parents because...well, I could not speak. Speaking for the first time was the greatest gift I ever had when I turned three. Then I had to learn to use words to communicate. I said a lot of things that didn't make sense. Maybe it was because I was excited with my new speech. But then I learned how to greet people by saying: "Hello. My name is Tyler; what is your name?" When I have said that to kids my age, all of them have just looked at me and then walked away quietly and slowly. I felt confused seeing them leave and disappointed because they never spoke to me or told me what their names were. I was confused and sad, but that has never stopped me from doing it again with whomever I meet. Now I usually say, "Hey, the name's McNamer; what's yours?" Most of the time, they respond with their own words, but sometimes, people don't know what to say. Just like when they were kids, I guess.

I have noticed that people communicate in a lot of ways besides words—using sign language, dance moves, eye contact or lack of it, body language, drawing, and writing. At first, I had no idea there were so many ways to communicate other than just using words or speaking in different languages. In high school, people around me say a lot of hurtful things to each other. It's no big surprise because it's high school in the twenty-first century. Because they all had the same sense of communication, I knew I was different from the entire school. My words were complex; I was quiet a lot of the time. I never feared anything about school (except homework), and I usually sat alone in school and walked around outside. What does that have to do with communication? In my thoughts, I communicated by saying, "I am different; I can't speak like you do; I am not interested in your mean words and stories."

Kids used to challenge me to do something I didn't want to do. They would do it in a sort of friendly way, like they were encouraging me to do it. One kid at the football game told me that I should go streaking in the football field. Instead of saying "No," I looked at the field and looked back at the kid and smiled, saying, "Come back to me when you are ready to speak for real!" Then I walked away without another word.

One time, a group of kids came to me, saying, "Hey, Tyler, this kid called you a name; he thinks you're dumb and wants to pummel ya." I responded by saying, "May I see this kid?" The group of kids looked excited as if they wanted to see a fight. I expected them to react that way, so when I saw the kid, I said, "Please don't say things about me." Then I walked away. It's always the walking away part that makes me have control of myself. I felt that I made up my own way of communicating by using self-control. My parents say that if you say "No" and walk away, you have more control of yourself. Having more control is the same as having power over yourself. It feels good. I don't see why kids don't defend themselves that way. They have told me that I'm a fool, an idiot, and a coward. But I tell them, "Only a fool would be cowardly enough not to have self-control. You idiots!" Then once again, I walk away. Sometimes, people who don't have self-control tend to get violent because of confusion. I had no words or desire to hurt anyone after taking my would-be attacker down; I did the same thing that I always like to do in situations like these. Walk away.

4

HIGH SCHOOL COURAGE

Rather than focus on my memories, I want to point out what's going on in the present for me in high school. I usually walk, run, or bike to school since I live so close by. I am not talking about me in this chapter... well sorta, but I am talking about how I view others around me and their energy. Once, I offered to play tennis on a sunny day at school with some kids, but no one wanted to play. Then I invited people to play cards with me during lunch; some of them played, but most of them did not. A few years later, no one wanted to play cards anymore. So I really had nothing to do during lunch after I ate, and I couldn't write more on this book because I wanted it to be a surprise to everyone. High school really is not the same as elementary school, when recess was the best thing that ever happened in school.

When I was a freshman in high school, kids thought the freshman year would be the worst year of high school. To be honest, I was quite nervous about being new to the school, but I never wanted to lose my courage before the whole campus. I showed that even a small freshman student can make the biggest and loudest roar for the Spartans, the name of our school team at Bainbridge. A very popular senior even encouraged me to do great things for the high school and had his friends join in the support. When that class of seniors graduated, I felt sad and alone. They had given me great appreciation and even made a club called "Tyler Rules!" It felt amazing. All because of the courage I showed that I cared for the seniors. I even wrote a letter in the school newspaper just to say goodbye to them.

During my freshman year, I wrote another newspaper article before the year ended. It was about the school dances and how they are not really dances at school. I showed a lot of courage by speaking up about what was going on. I was prepared for being hated by everyone who liked the dirty dances, but I did it, and a revolution has been going on since I posted that article. Here is the article I wrote:

LET'S FIX OUR DANCES, BHS!
TYLER MCNAMER
GUEST REPORTER
DANCE ENTHUSIAST

I love to dance! Dancing is one of the things I like to do for fun. But when it comes to school dances, I begin to lose my dancing spirit. It all started at the last dance I went to. It was the end of the basketball season and all the fans had gone wild cheering for the BHS Spartans. To celebrate, we went to the dance where the fans got a chance to move around just as much as the basketball players moved around. In the commons, it was dark, lights were everywhere, the DJs were playing music, and the whole crowd filled up the dance floor. As I was dancing, something didn't seem right. There was rap music and people doing dirty dancing. I heard a report not long ago that kids drink and smoke outside the commons. No wonder most of the kids never want to dance. That's just my thought. With that, I left the dance for good.

Dancing is all about having fun and moving with your hands, feet, hips, and your whole body. When I read a dictionary, Rap is defined as a talk, conversation, or discussion in music. Out of all the dances I have been to for weddings, parties, and other celebrations, I have to say that high school nowadays is not a safe place to dance. Personally, I'm trying to show my BHS spirit when I dance. I have a hard time talking to people at lunch. To show my high school spirit and have fun with my classmates, I dance. To me, dancing is a language through which you can speak with your body, but not with your tongue.

So if you like smoking, drinking alcohol, and doing dirty dancing as if you're in a nightclub, why don't you come up with your own club off-campus?

Building a dance party is simple, with 5 easy steps.

Step 1: Have an open space to dance.

Step 2: Put up the lights.

Step 3: Use a D.J. turntable to play music.

Step 4: Dance like crazy!

Step 5: Clean up afterward.

At Union Grove High School in a suburb of Milwaukee, Wisconsin, there are strict rules for school dances. The thing that bothers me most at BHS dances is what Union Grove calls "Sexual Bending." It bothers me because I don't think it has much to do with dancing. Almost everyone does it. I come to dances to dance. Those who do this "Sexual Bending" stuff would immediately get kicked out of a dance for good if they were at Union Grove High. In my opinion, kids have more fun dancing without doing the "Sexual Bending" routine. As a matter of fact, "bending" can lead kids to be sexually active, and that leads to danger!

I have done interviews with Ms. Duvall, Ms. Lemmon, and Mr. Peterson and talked to them about what goes on inside dances. Ms. Duvall said that dancing was really different back when she was in high school, when there was none of that bending stuff. "I'm not a fan of this dirty dancing routine. Dances should be fun and safe," said Duvall. I then talked to Ms. Lemmon and Mr. Peterson about the same topic. Both agreed with Duvall, saying that the type of music in school dances tempts kids to do the "grinding" stuff. When my freshmen friends and I were in 8th grade, we had strict rules for our dances. But now that we are in high school, freshmen feel that they are free to dance however they want, following the example of kids in higher grades. According to Ms. Lemmon, more kids are showing up intoxicated at school dances than ever before. "Those who are drunk or high are handed over to the police and are suspended from school for 10 days," said Ms. Lemmon. I then asked Mr. Peterson why, besides the music, he thinks kids dance like this. "Kids are influenced by older kids at BHS and even TV," commented Peterson. I know what he means. The higher the grade, the more influence they have on the grade below. For example, seniors influence juniors, juniors influence sophomores, and sophomores influence freshmen. The administration is going to talk to the disc jockeys at dances and ask them to change the music to make it less tempting for students to grind and bend. In school dances, everyone hears a lot of rap, and rap is the music that tempts kids to grind. Dancing is dancing, grinding is grinding, and bending is bending; you simply can't combine them. Rap is just talking. I'm not a talking person, I'M A DANCING PERSON!

Perhaps kids don't have courage to come up with dance moves. They were too lame at least to learn how to do a disco pose. They think that even the simplest provocative set of moves would be cool. Maybe they believe that everyone can be cool once they do these moves. I have been told that if I sexually bend, I would be cool like everyone else. I have my own style; I don't take advice from my peers. Once again, I walk away from these situations. I know I cannot change everyone's behavior since I'm just a kid, but I can change the future of school dances for Bainbridge. It takes so much courage to:

Point out the problem.

Walk away from situations in the dances.

Write out an article about the dances and start a revolution, and

Take the hurtful comments and move on.

The article became so popular that even the Bainbridge Island press wrote a report and sent the news all over the island.

Kids thought I was crazy to take everything hurtful that was said to me and make it look like not a big deal. In my head, a big deal is when you go to jail for a long time. I was never afraid of threats from kids my age. What were they going to do? Tell on me for what I have been doing? That could happen, but what does that do? It just tells people I have been doing good.

Funny stuff happens to those who don't agree with me. Brawlers tend to think that fists are the answer to make me change my opinion. In this situation, the only question that always comes into my head is: "Does my enemy have the skills to punch his enemy without being ready to dodge or block?" I fight for my own defense, never in offense. When I was attacked by a bunch of "protesters," yet another form of courage was born in me. After my enemy was down and hurt, the kids cheered for me, but I didn't say anything. A long pause occurred, making the watchers wonder in confusion. I left after the silence, knowing that my enemy could heal by himself without any noise. I never ask for fights. I never wanted to hurt anyone.

Courage is a great thing to have; it makes you feel like you can do anything legal. Illegal courage will make you feel trapped. For example, if you have the "courage" to try meth, you will feel trapped in your head. Or if you have the "courage" to rob a bank, you will feel trapped in jail. The courage to do good things is the best kind of courage to have in my opinion. I guess America has so much freedom that people also have the freedom to be trapped.

You know what else I have the courage to do? Write this book for you to read.

5

TORTURED BY BULLIES

Mentally and physically, bullies literally have been a part of my life.

Since preschool, I have been bullied. I don't blame others for what they have done to me. After all, I was entirely different from everyone in school. In my mind, I felt like an alien throughout the years and literally tried to take off the "mask" that's really my face when I was little. In preschool, I never learned how to have fun with others. I was more serious until I discovered how to have fun at recess during first grade. Even though I then began to play with others, the bullies just kept coming.

I was punched, kicked, and thrown to the ground by kids because I was so different. It was a shame that I couldn't remember names back then, and I still have trouble with names sometimes now. Each year I was bullied. Even when the bullies stopped, eventually new ones would show up.

I honestly don't blame the bullies for what they've done to me. It is never right to treat others like trash, but it did teach me lessons. Lessons that include how one world can be cruel to another world by throwing asteroids at one another. Why do people act this way? I think it is from boredom or they just want to be higher than anyone else. To me, that's a lame way to get "higher than anyone else" because bullies are just mean to every-one. That really makes them lower than everyone because they are the biggest losers in school.

Even when bullied, I always stood up for myself and treated people nicely and with kindness. But sadly enough, the bullies kept coming at me and picking on me. It was when I was in fifth grade that I took my stand to defend myself and take down the bullies. This part is hard to imagine for me, but I punched, kicked, and threw my opponents down to the ground. My first words to them were "How does it feel to be treated like trash?" Then I walked away. Fighting like that is very hard for me because I never wanted to hurt anybody and those memories of fighting others are stuck in my head. They drive me crazy when I think about them. And even worse, the kids expected me to fight again. I made it clear that I never wanted to fight, only for self-defense. I guess I learned a good lesson after that time I defended myself in the fifth grade. When people stand up for themselves, it can make more bullies come after them. A new way to become popular I sadly would say.

When I learned more about the whole 9/11 terrorist attack on the Twin Towers during first grade, I learned that even adults can be big bullies. At the time, I was thinking, "When will this torture end?" It almost seems like it will never end. September 11, 2001 was an important year for us. I never thought it could be that big of a deal.

Many times I have felt like my favorite comic book hero, Superman. When I wrote that article about why school dances were bad, I felt like Superman because I was able to have one of his powers—self-control. So many people have hated me for what I've done and who I am. Like I said before, I don't blame them for hating me because of my unique way of seeing things; I was glad I said something about the school dances. Because I was brave and stood up strong, it inspired the seniors, juniors, and even the sophomores, and it gave me great honor for my action. The older people gave me praise, but the freshmen gave me the hardest time. They thought I was crazy and tried to beat me up just to make themselves look good. It was funny because I remember a couple of seniors defended me! It was awesome! They were kind enough to take me to the principal's office and tell him what happened. Everything went smoothly after that.

Whenever I fight in self-defense, it really hurts me to hurt anyone else. It's like my dad's theory—he would spank me so hard that I wouldn't feel my butt for days, and all the time, he never liked it, but he had to teach me a lesson. As for me, when I defend myself, I keep thinking of Dad when doing it because I know I need to teach my enemies a lesson, so I punish them as hard as I can until they give up.

There was a time when I almost did not forgive myself for this behavior. I was at a football game when this streaker hit me in the head before going streaking on the field. After he did that, I grabbed him and punched him so hard I knocked him out. Everyone expected me to feel pity for an action like that, but instead, I took out my phone and called an ambulance... and an officer too. That person was arrested for disturbing the peace. Disturbing my peace, that is; people can't hit people and streak during a ball game. Surely it taught him a lesson just like I'd hoped. Still though, I didn't want him to ruin the band's performance. It was very brave of me to stop him and call the authorities, but sometimes, that moment has bothered me for some reason. Maybe it's because of that knockout punch I did on him.

That's the thing about emotions. They are very dangerous when released. When I became a sophomore, people bullied me even more. I hated it. So one day, when I was at an assembly, my thoughts about being bullied were bashing around in my head. When those thoughts were in my head, my emotions were released. I SCREAMED in rage, I cried with tears, and I even laughed hysterically, thinking "How weak people are against me!" I was self-named "Terror Tyler." When I was calm, I called myself "Tame Tyler." Then when I was a junior, I thought to myself, "Man, I should never call myself two names. I'm just Tyler." With all those emotions being released, that's when things get dangerous like when I knocked out the streaker. I am proud that I left the rest of that job to the authorities. That's when I learned self-control. My theory is that anyone can be the craziest freak in the world, *and* anyone can be the calmest person in the world. Which person do you want to be? If I were you, I'd be the second dude. Releasing emotions can happen anywhere. But the best place to release it all is in a lonely place, or releasing them mentally with family members.

It sure is strange for me to see people make big deals out of small hits. I remember when I was six, I played laser tag, and I got knocked over by a bunch of teenagers. Instead of crying, I got up and continued playing, as if it had never happened. Same with soccer—some people would kick me in the shin and trip me sometimes by accident, and I would keep on going. Personally, I don't call in the fouls when the physical stuff happens to me; instead, I will move on easily and keep playing. Unfortunately, a lot of people whine and stop the games just because of small things. One time, I accidentally kicked someone's shins and he tripped. He made a big deal about his shins and I apologized.

Then things got ridiculous. I said, "Get up! You are not special; you're just a strong athlete." And then I kept playing and scored the goals. Sometimes, even whiners can be bullies because they make me into the bad guy, which I'm not.

When I view people as "not special," I mean that they are not "handicapped" or (forgive me) "retarded." Although I like the name "special" for those with special needs. In my mind, it's the people who treat each other poorly; they are the ones who are retarded. I've learned that I am nothing special. I like the label "gifted." Sounds good to me.

Throughout my life, I have been mentally beat up by a lot of people. When it comes to my family, they "shift" me mentally, but sometimes in a harsh way. I say "shift me mentally" because anyone can change over time, usually through interaction with others. You know, shifting to make better choices. My family are the only ones who shift me or better yet move me (unless if it's teachers or coaches who know my family, if you know what I mean). But as for everyone else who is the same age as me, I'm never like any of them. I have had the ability to gain power over them because I am so different from them. My mom and dad were literally adults when they were in school—smart, isolated, and well-controlled. With my parents' genetics and my autism, I felt extremely isolated and different. I got used to it. There was a time when I got so used to the isolation that I had a dream that everyone on earth was replaced by clones of myself. We ruled the world all together. Felt good at the time, until I learned that everything would be boring and not entertaining if we were all the same.

I hate bullies, but yet they have helped me in a way. They helped me to realize how people can be so mean and cruel to one another, even when they grow up to be adults. From them, I have learned how to stand tall and proud. By saying that, I mean that I have learned not to change who I am because of other kids. What I did not want to learn is defending with force. I felt like I had to, however, because of my defense strategy; the kids then viewed me as a weapon, an unstoppable force that went against giants. After hearing those things about me, I did not view the comments as good, so when I heard them from kids, I said nothing and walked away. I never wanted to be a weapon or a force. Instead, I think, "Why can't everyone just leave me alone?" It's a common feeling for a lot of people. I can see why.

In conclusion, I've noticed that good people are the ones who get bullied the most, but when a bully bullies another bully, that makes it fun for both of them; that's why there are wars between people every day.

6

DREAMS

A dream is like the creation of the moon. Once that dream comes true, it orbits around my world. When the dream does not come true, it becomes a comet speeding throughout the galaxy. I would say that I have fifty-seven moons orbiting my world, big and small. Countless numbers of comets shoot out from my world. It is beautiful to see them because dreams can be the ideal of imagination.

Sleep itself is one of the most mysterious things in the world. When you close your eyes, you try to go to sleep by getting comfortable. At first, you just stay awake, and then the next thing you know, it's morning. In real life, sleep is so quick, but in the dream world, it's a whole new adventure.

One of my dreams that came true was about riding my bike around Bainbridge Island. It felt great, just like in the dream. Another dream that came true and goes in orbit in my world is flying. Flying a plane that is. I never before felt so great being up in high places like I did flying in a plane and seeing how small things were below me.

They say that dreams mean something to the sleeper. To me, every dream has meaning. The meaning is imagination. Then, hopefully, if the dream is possible, it can be done in real life.

One day I had a dream about my grandfather, Alfred, or Grandpa Al as we call him. I was in the front lines of the Vietnam War with him. I heard him say, "War is fuel; you get more of that natural high every time you kill, and you will be the most invincible man with great determination. Now get out there, Tiger, and get that natural high!" In my dream, I did what he said: be a part of war. I did not like it. By the time I pulled that trigger, I woke up from that nightmare. I started to think what he meant by "natural high" when I was little. Then it came to me that determination for anything makes you get that natural high. Drugs are for those who don't know how to find the natural high. That natural high is called adrenalin.

My other dreams seem interesting and feel like they make the most sense because they relate to my surroundings. One time I dreamed that I was running on buildings and then jumped, falling to the ground, but I kept falling after I hit the ground. I then landed on a new city, a city that was all broken down, run-down, and dark looking. There were kids from my school there who were not nice and even tried to attack me. But then I had a force field shield blocking them from touching me. I began to see something bright and walked slowly toward it. As I walked, I saw the troubles that were going on in this dark area. The kids followed me and said hurtful things about events that had happened during my days at school. But still, I kept on walking, ignoring them. As I reached the end of the dark gray area, I saw flower petals being carried by the wind. I thought they were going to be something big when I first saw how bright they were, but they turned out to be flowers. The flowers later led me to green grass. I looked at the dark city; then I looked at the green grass. I walked through the green grass and fell asleep. I woke up moments later in my bed. I was eight years old when I dreamed that dream.

A little while later, I had the same dream, but with a different ending. I was still in the rundown city with the kids everywhere being bad. But instead of walking just forward, I stopped in the middle of the havoc and looked around me while everyone was being rude to me. I just stood there doing nothing. They tried everything they could to get rid of me, but I had my shield still intact. Then they tried ignoring me, but I stayed there. When I was little, I believed that everyone had a good side. Too bad it didn't turn out that way in the real world. As I stayed there, people around me asked, "Why are you here?" I replied, "I'm here to ask you this: Why are you doing these things?" The people around me were silent and had no answer. Then I smiled because I had talked to people.

I was trying to figure out that dream for a while; then it hit me. In the city, enough is never enough. In the grass, all you need is flowers and sunlight. Nature seems simple; it never gets old, and it never gets upgraded. The kids in my school, however, want the newer stuff like the electronic iPads and all that "i" stuff. If I were to rename the product, I would call it "i-solation." I've always wanted to go to a field where it's nothing but grass and flowers. I would then feel like the whole world belongs to me. I wouldn't be isolated because I connect with the fresh air and the field itself. Just for one day. The part about falling from buildings means to me that eventually I'm going to fall when doing something I love, for example running.

When it comes to dreams, everything is possible, not necessarily in real life, but in sleep. That's why whenever I wake up, I think, "Oh man!" because the dream is over. I can't dream forever because that would hold me back from reality. Sometimes, you can mix dreams with reality. For instance, when I was a freshman, I dreamed of becoming a homecoming prince for the freshman grade. That dream came true. I treasure it always.

There is one last dream I want to share in this book. I had a dream that everyone in the galaxy can understand my world. Maybe even the unknown universe. This dream has become a comet. I hope that it slowly becomes a moon.

7

LOOKING CONFIDENT

It is normal for someone who is different to look at himself and discover why he is different. For me, almost everything made me different—my face, eyebrows, hair, voice, and even my own name. I felt like my name was not right, especially if my first and last name rhymed. I never changed my name, but I still had my doubts back then. I look in the mirror almost every time I see one anywhere just to see how I look. It's funny because when my parents see me looking in the mirror, my mom will say, "If you're ugly, then your mom and dad are ugly as well." My parents are very beautiful. Then my dad will say, "You look great; I'll tell you if you ain't."

Even though the nicest things may be said to you, you still pay attention to the smaller things like your voice, or how thin you are. I was not born big, but I have always thought that if you were born big in weight, then you would be stronger and be even more attractive. This doesn't mean eating burgers 24/7, but big as in born to develop big muscles. It's all in the genes.

I have experienced a lot of things that have urged me to change my identity, but my mind told me, "If you change your looks, you change your heart." I randomly say a lot of things in the present that I don't mean to. This saying in my head really triggered me at the time. If I changed my voice to a deeper tone, people would not recognize me and would think I'm some sort of monster. Not really good for my heart. If I changed my face like one of those plastic surgeries, same thing; I would not be recognized, and be known as a monster. If I were to change my name, no one, not even my parents would know me because they were the ones who named me. I would be exhausted telling everyone why I changed my name. But nicknames on the other hand are all right with me. I know I have heard this saying, "Ugly on the outside, but beautiful on the inside." So what's the point of making a change on the outside when you have others saying that you're a great looking man? Of course, this doesn't mean I don't have to change my clothes or have my hair cut, but you get the picture.

When I came to this realization, I made a change in myself to be more confident and courageous with my looks. I became more open to my best friends about how great I look. It's the way I joke around with my friends. Sometimes having the courage to believe in your good looks makes you a very popular kid. That's my view of things, even if it's not yours.

8

"HI, TYLER!"

Throughout my whole life, I have communicated with others in the world. The world seems to like to say two words to me a lot of the time. Those words bring a smile to my face every day.

Those words are "Hi, Tyler." Every day at elementary, intermediate, middle, and high school, my peers would say, "Hi, Tyler" to me. It's not a complex sentence; it's not simple...well, yes, it is, but I feel like when my peers say it to me, they are telling me a lot of things in my mind. They might say "Hey, Tyler, nice shirt" or "Good luck on that test," or anything positive like that. I even expressed my feelings from those words to one person by saying: "I compliment you for saying 'Hi.' I give you my 'Hi' back; keep up the good work." It was worth saying that to him, and I gave him a quarter.

It had been so long since "Hi, Tyler" became a huge deal for me. Then I realized that it seemed like it was only me who gets the "Hi, Tyler." Yes, it's probably the whole autism thing, but why can't I be just like one of them? Even though it is very sweet for them to say "Hi" to me, it also made me feel less special because it doesn't seem the same as what the other people go through when it comes to communication with each other. Either way, it still is nice for them to notice me.

This chapter may be short, but it's worth writing about because communication, even if it's just saying "Hi," is an important part of my life.

9

GROWING PALMS

About the same time people get the chance to take their first breaths, they get their first chance to grab ahold of something. That something is a parent's finger. We all grow up and still hold our parents' hands. Every year, our hands get bigger and bigger. To me, my hands are a sign of growing older. Every time I look at my hands, I see that they are not baby hands; they are big and useful hands. When a baby grabs hold of my finger, I see myself as an infant again. I see that my hands are not small anymore. Thinking about being an infant gives me the chills every time because memories makes me sad since I can't relive them.

I hear the saying "Let it go" a lot of times, but it's hard to let it go sometimes. We can let go of the past, but we can't let go of the heart. When my heart and mind are focused on the past, it's super hard to let go. That doesn't mean I can't move on with my life, but sometimes, just sometimes, it's good to relive those moments from the past.

As a teenager, it's hard to deal with acne and all the changes of growing into an adult. I personally think that when I was a child, I was viewed as being at my cutest, and now I'm just seen as a regular teenager. But that doesn't move me from my confidence in being a good-looking boy overall.

Grabbing stuff and lifting stuff is another way of knowing that you're growing older. First the light things, then the heavier things. I know this difference is obvious since I go to a gym and work out there.

I view a person's palms as a growing subject because they sometimes show what has become of a person. In my high school, there have been a lot of drunks and stoners. Whenever an incident took place, I would view the person as he or she was an infant. Then I can never see a beer bottle or a joint in the person's hand. It's never possible for any infant to have such things in his or her hands. Then I see the person in the present doing drugs and driving while drinking and all that sort of nonsense. The palms of their hands show what their choices are and what are the purposes of those choices. I know I'm not a parent, but that's just the way I see things like that.

I once looked at my hand just to see whether there were any spots from falling onto dirt after tripping. I then clenched my hand till it made a fist, but then came an old leaf that fell on my hand, and I crunched it, making that crunching sound. It was then that I saw myself old with the crunched up leaf that had the same color as my skin. Once I cleansed my hand, it was normal again. In my mind, growing old in looks doesn't always mean that I can stay a child at heart. Washing away the leaf means that being a child is possible; being old is an excuse not to have a little child in me. It will be the chance to be stronger and have more power. Having thoughts of the past shows everyone that I care for the past and that I had a very good life in the past, making me feel good about letting all the good things come out, and even letting all the sad things come out. It is always important to care about the present because there would not be any past without a present, and without a present, there will never be a future. Thinking about the future also is good because there are expectations in doing so.

I may look into a mirror and see myself through the reflection. When there is no reflection around me, I look at the palms of my hands, and see how much I've grown.

10

HEALING WOUNDS

It's a "no duh" moment when everybody has troubles that need to be solved. So many troubles can affect each individual person, and they are all part of life. But there are a lot of people who just cannot face the fact of life, so they use as much effort as they can to escape it. Drinking alcohol and taking drugs are two main activities I think of when people want to escape. People can't be alcoholics forever, but the people who take bad drugs seem to be saying to me three words: "I give up!"

In my school, a lot of people have taken drugs and will drink until they are weaker than an injured dog. One of my senior friends was drinking and driving and died after a high school graduation party. In my opinion, alcohol parties are also a sign of giving up because people don't know how to be themselves when partying. So they rely on liquor. You don't have to agree; I'm just pointing out what seems understandable to me. What makes sense to me.

People always want that "buzz" feeling to make them "feel good" so they can escape. Having too much of a good thing is like having so much candy that it can make you sick. Like with a snobbish brat who wants more, no good will ever come from trying to make that brat happy. Same with drugs; no good will ever come after wanting more of that drug. It's very expensive to live on Bainbridge Island. When parents are rich, their kids think they can get anything they want, whenever they want, and nothing will ever happen to them, no matter what. I don't view my parents as being "rich" in money or anything like that. I view them neutrally and just as regular parents who love and care for their child.

It is the same thing when it comes to kids joining the army, navy, or any other branch of the military. It's like what my dad said when I was ten: "If you have no future, go join the military." My two grandfathers joined the military, and it sure affected their lives in very bad ways. I may be tough, but I never want to take people's lives away or help others to do so. When I was a freshman, I had some senior friends who decided to join the military; then after three years, I heard reports of their injuries, and now some can't walk anymore. It clearly is a bad career to take, especially when you have kids.

Kids were probably never happy being on Bainbridge Island, even being in a place where the schools are among the top ten in the country. During high school, relationships start evolving and when things go insane, hard times occur. Family matters sometimes don't go very well. Kids want to rebel against their parents and do whatever they want to do with friends. Of course, things happen when it comes to high school, but like every choice, there are always consequences. Good or bad.

I think kids don't really want their parents to help them anymore, so they do whatever they can to get away from them. Drinking, drugs, or even going to their friends' houses are all ways they try to escape. There is nothing wrong with asking a friend's advice, but it's always better in my opinion to have a family member help a kid.

The reason why I called this chapter "Healing Wounds" is because in all the fights I've been in, I taught myself that if I get hurt, I must always heal myself naturally. Let the body heal itself without any help. If my enemy is defeated, he must learn to suffer from his own mistake of attacking a random person just to fight for fun. Same thing with life, one must learn from one's mistakes, and let his own wounds heal. Someone (and that includes everyone) may feel lost, confused, sad, upset, or hopeless in the world we live in.

All my life, I have made bad mistakes that drove my parents crazy. I had so much self-discipline and ego that most of the time I didn't want my parents' advice. One day, I climbed on the roof of my elementary school and got in big trouble for doing so. I was curious to see what was on my school's roof. My parents' attitude toward me was all "I told you so," but they didn't really say that out loud. Admitting my wounds to my family members helps them to heal faster. It feels good too. Then my parents told me about how many mistakes they made when they were kids. It is good to have your wounds healed more quickly by loved ones, but if challenges come to people with no help at all, healing your wounds by yourself is how to become stronger in the heart.

I have seen teen dramas on TV or in the movies where the kids tell their parents, "You just don't get it; nobody gets it" and they run upstairs crying. To me, I find such drama scenes kind of funny because they are just an excuse for saying, "I want to do this, and no one should judge me." Of course, there are family members who "get it" and understand what's going on. Family members were once kids too; that fact is something that the kids don't get. I sure want to see a parent say, "You just don't get it; nobody gets it" and run upstairs, crying "dramatically." That would make a good comedy sitcom.

As I was saying, everyone makes mistakes, but it's the recovery that makes everyone strong.

11

DISCOVERING AUTISM

When I was ten, I discovered that I had autism. My parents had a long conversation with me about it. A whole lot of feelings then came over me in an intense way. I started feeling angry, depressed, confused, impatient, and isolated. I expressed it so intensely that I started hurting people physically and mentally. For a long time, I tried really hard to fit in and hide my autism by observing what other people were doing. I literally tried to fit into their world and be like them. But I have reasoned out now that I cannot be like everyone else. I cannot think like everyone else. So that is why most of the time, I never take anyone's advice, unless it's someone I trust dearly like my family members.

I have been to places where they have the "special" kids expressing themselves through talking, movement, artwork, and any of those activities where the adults talked slowly and simply to us. Those places made me feel bad. I literally felt like I had no future and would never grow up. For a while, I thought it was cool because I never wanted to grow up, but being around those kids seemed different compared to being around other kids. I do know that they are special all right, not in a retarded way, but in a very special way. I would wonder why I was in those places? Was there something wrong with me? Was I stupid? What was my purpose in being autistic? I then came to the conclusion that "special" was not me. I was self-proclaimed as "gifted" and not special.

Then after all those activities where I was treated like a small child (in my opinion), I noticed that people were being nice to me in my middle and high school. I was accepted in nice and kind ways when the kids were around me, but when they talked to each other, except when with me, they would talk bad and be hurtful to one another. It seems like when I am there, they are nice to me and say short phrases like "Hey, Tyler!" or "How's the football game?" I respond with a hello back and an accurate statement of what was the score, but then the conversation ends. Even though I try to continue the conversation by asking how their weeks were, they seem to say just short words like "Fine."

My observation about kids my age is that they really treat each other differently compared to when they see me. It's like they have a new language that communicates to me but not their own language.

When I was in preschool, I would not be a part of what kids were doing like playing games. I usually just sat in the corner and watched. In my mind, I thought the kids would invite me to play, and not the teacher, but I expected too much—they were kids. When I was little, I expected a lot of stuff, and 85 percent of the time it never happened. With that extra 15 percent, I was ready to be a part of what I always hoped would be.

In elementary school, I was too serious and strict. I used to look at classical composers from the past. Beethoven was my favorite and still is; I was so into his profile and music that most of the time at the computer lab, I enjoyed looking at *World Book* and learning more about him, or in the library, I would look at an encyclopedia.

As a kid, I was always wondering how things work and why they work like that. I was curious about a soccer ball. I caught it out of mid-air and a kid shouted "handball." Another kid said, "Over here!" But I bounced it and then tried to kick it to the kids. Sadly, I kicked it over my head and down the hill by the elementary school. Kids were angry with me and went down to get it while calling me names. Luckily, the teachers saved the day, and I apologized to the kids, and they apologized to me. It's just that the ball was fun to play with; I had a ball with that ball.

After knowing that I had autism, I had flashbacks of my past. I regretted everything that I did. I was strict, weird, confused, and even thought I was stupid. My parents told me I was not stupid; I was just curious about almost everything I saw and that I was different than the other kids. They told me that I had autism.

After reviewing the times when I was a little lad, in a way I felt I was more mature than any of my peers. I thought outside the box, I was focused on goals, and I also had an amazing memory, and I still have that memory today. Since my parents were serious and mature during their school days, I was like them.

Autism is not an excuse to be different. I have tried to be like everyone in the world, but it never works out the way I want it to, ever! No one can think the way I do. Having autism is like being a regular person, but the only powerful part that's different to the world is the mind. Having a mind that views the world differently is a new experience for everyone. If you know anyone with autism, let him or her talk to you so you can try to understand what's going on in that person's mind. Autistic people are here for some reason. Let's see if you can find that reason.

12

I HATE DIVORCE!

Yeah, yeah, yeah. My parents are divorced. Stinks, right? Saying it out loud makes it feel better. Thinking about it is the hard part. I will be strong and tell you what the divorce was like and how it affected me.

When my dad left my mom, he took all the good stuff. Mostly our biggest TV in the house. I still don't know why he did that. I guess it's one of those selfish things people do. He remarried a woman. I did not like the whole scene. It made me think about why my dad, Jody, left my mom, Kristina. In my own head, I came up with ten reasons why:

1. Dad never wanted to work together as a team.
2. Mom is ugly.
3. It's never his way all the time.
4. Because Mom is so annoying.
5. No one should get any of Dad's money.
6. He never wanted to figure stuff out.
7. He felt trapped in our family.
8. Dad never wanted to share a laugh with the family.
9. My dad thinks he doesn't need me and my mom in his life.
10. Dad would never want to see me grow up and spend time together with him every day.

None of the things I thought were true, but at least I said them in my mind. I was eight years old when Dad left. It didn't mean I would never see him ever again. I got to see him in Tacoma. Then he moved again to Gig Harbor.

Later on, I learned that my stepmom was pregnant and was going to have a baby boy. I became absolutely FURIOUS with rage! I did not explain my anger to my dad because I thought you were supposed to be happy for a pregnant woman. All my life, I had thought I was going to be the only son in the family. I wanted to stay with Mom forever, but I needed to see my dad too at some time. I hated Dad, while I was over there. I wasn't the most well-behaved child when I went to their home for a visit.

Then one day in the car, my dad brought up the whole divorce subject. I did not want to talk about it at all. But I told him everything I felt about the whole situation. At that time, I did not feel any better because I felt that talking to my dad wasn't enough. Then out of nowhere, at a different time in the car, my Stepmom brought up the subject. She told me everything about the reasons for divorce and how she understood it was hard for me. I made a better connection with her after that.

With Mom, it was hard being with her and her pain. I could never understand why this separation happened, but it sure did affect both of us as if a bomb had been dropped from the sky. I don't even want to understand it now; I feel like it's not worth knowing.

Then, however, I could never hold back the feeling of questioning. Why did it all happen for real? All my life I had known I was a planned child. I was created on purpose. My mom and dad craved the day when I would come into their lives. Both of them loved me equally. It was almost as if they would never leave me ever. By the time the separation was complete, I knew I was rejected from the heart. I hated everything Dad did, and I hoped that he would regret everything he did. But it was too late for a remarriage. Work took over my dad and his new wife. I had a feeling that they married because they shared a common interest: Work. I understand that it provides for the family, but for me, work doesn't affect anything but money for the "family." If money is so important when it comes to businesses, then I always wonder whether it's possible to do something *with* the family instead of working for the family. I had that theory for a long time when I was a kid, so I didn't want Dad's money whenever he offers it to me.

After the divorce, Mom used to have panic attacks and I wouldn't know what to do. Life was hard for me. I had to be in two different worlds, and I had to act differently in both worlds. I was young when I wanted to cheer up Mom.

This situation never meant that I was going to be sad forever. Eventually, I formed a close connection with Dad, his wife, and my brother. I have that same kind of connection with my mom too. Dad and Mom still work together so I can see both of them on certain weekends. When it comes to their teamwork, I feel really good because while I know they are divorced, they both still have a good connection reflected in their teamwork. Once that teamwork was established, everything began to go well for all of us.

Sometimes, however, I feel like I have to put on a different personality depending on when I am at Dad's house or Mom's house. With Mom, I'm all goofy and full of energy, ready to let it all out. With Dad, I'm more serious and I worry about making mistakes. With Mom, I feel like I can be myself around her. It's like I'm alone and no one would care about my goofy behavior. My mom knows that I would not act goofy in public but I will at home. When it comes to Dad, I feel like I'm in public. Dad is a very good businessman; in fact, I view him as a dude who does great business, so I thought I should change my ways from being goofy to being serious. I kind of try to be a perfectionist when with Dad, but the more I try, the more I fail and disappoint. After all, he always says, "Son, you are perfect just the way you are." Those words will stay with me forever. The only person I can be goofy with at my dad's house is my brother. He's like Mom sometimes. He doesn't tell me what to do, but he sure likes almost the same things my mom and I like. But then I "accidentally" show him stuff like Chris Farley because I keep forgetting about his age.

The cool part about having two houses is the extra days going snowboarding. Shortly after I'm done snowboarding with Dad at Crystal Mountain, Mom takes me snowboarding on Mt. Hood in Oregon. Snowboarding is what I did while I was in Portland, Oregon during my winter breaks visiting my mormor.

Whenever I'm at Dad's, my brother always wants to do something with me since I'm not there as much. Whenever something is planned, my brother is always like "What about Tyler?" I think that is awesome. I want to do cool things with them too when there is nothing new to do at Mom's place. There are always things to do at both houses. It is like an adventure. But no one would ever have positive feeling from their parents getting divorced. All right! I got that out of my head, but to make me feel even better, I'll say it again. I HATE DIVORCE!

13

BALANCE AND MOODS

When I was little, I always wanted things to be equal. If I spun to the left, I would also spin to the right. If I rolled forward, I would roll backward. If I pointed with my index finger, I would point with my ring finger and the same with my other hand. Back then, I used almost everything with my middle finger. I did not get it from anything or anyone. I was still a little kid back then so I did not know what it really meant to show someone the middle finger.

Kids thought I was weird when I wanted things to be equal. Not a big surprise to me, but I couldn't help trying to get things equal with my body. It's like I couldn't have anything "different." I'm not like that today, even though I do think left should come first after right, but that's only me.

Probably the reason why I don't pay much attention to having things in balance anymore is because of my right broken leg, and my bent right ring finger. I hated everything about my bent finger, not only because of the pain, but that it doesn't look the same as my left side. Then I realized that it's hard to notice and people don't mind things like that.

I may have had things in "balance" back in the day, but there's something else that did get way "off balance." That's my mood.

I was once the most serious kid in the whole school who never learned how to have fun. Maybe it's because my parents were divorced. Maybe it's because I couldn't figure out why I'm so different. There were a lot of ideas on why I never learned how to have fun.

When I look back, I remember how serious I was and how I wasn't very fun back in the day even as I grew older. I could never forgive myself for my behavior back then, so I wanted to make up for it by trying to be the most fun boy in the school. It felt great being in a better mood. Wait...was I trying to do that balancing thing again? I think I was, wasn't I? I guess I was balancing my moods. I never thought of that before writing this chapter. That's the thing about writing; you never know what will come into your head. It's like drawing; you never know what you're going to draw next.

After I had my fun times, I went right back into being serious again. In middle and high school, I got into many fights with other kids. To be quite honest, I have a combination of being serious and having fun at the same time. I get serious when defending myself; then I have fun taunting my opponents for making their first moves on me. If you are the attacker and then lose to your victim, you become the biggest idiot on the planet. But then I learned, according to Dad, that these kinds of conflicts are never fun. When there is a fight between my two moods, the serious side always gets the edge. I have been treated badly by others over the school years, and because of that, I learned not to trust anyone, except for my parents and teachers and all the trusted adults around me. But I never trusted anyone who was my age in high school. That lack of trust is one of the reasons why I am so confident about myself. I had that attitude where it is always going to be my way and nobody will change me. It felt great and fun feeling that way. Much freedom comes from that feeling I would say.

I guess I am still the same as when I was little, wanting things the same and equal. Not so much in terms of spinning around and such, but equal more in terms of moods, and weights while working out. I am never trying to force myself to be happy or sad and such, but there are times when I am sad and times when I am happy. Either way, it seems like a balance to me.

Whenever I see kids at school, they don't seem to be bright themselves. By bright, I mean "brightly colored." When I say brightly colored, I mean they all seem gray and not active or jumpy. I see them happy at times, but they don't use that joy by running or jumping. Of course, I'm not saying that they should do that. For me, when I'm happy, I can do almost anything in the world. That's how I became the "spirit" of Bainbridge Island—by showing school spirit through inspiring kids to be loud and active at sporting events.

14

IDENTITIES

Everyone has an identity. It explains who the person is and who he/she is supposed to be. My dad, Jody, has the identity called "Dad." So I call him Dad. Same with Kristina; I call her "Mom." Back when I was eight, I used to call my stepmom "C." I can't believe I just remembered that.

When I was little, I thought that names didn't really matter and that I would call people by their identity names. For example: uncles, aunts, friends, and strangers. I would even call people "friends" at school and the teacher "teacher." To tell the difference between my friends, I would say "Friend One," or "Friend Two" and so on.

Of course, that brought a lot of confusion and unfairness to people because they wanted to know who was number one. It wasn't until I was six years old that I started to call people by their names. I was used to calling my family members "Mom," "Dad," and so on, but it was the people outside my family whose names I needed to use. In my mind, I thought people who had identities like that were meant to be trusted. People who don't have identities are nobodies. Of course, that's not true, but I thought like that when I was younger. I learned that trust can be earned through effort by anyone. It just takes time, and that's the reason why family members are so trustworthy most of the time.

In school, I like to call almost everyone my "acquaintance" because I have a hard time remembering names. I usually would say "my fellow acquaintances" when I talked to people around my table during lunch. People thought I was weird, but I had to say something other than "Frank" or some other random name that wasn't theirs.

In writing this book, I identified you as the reader. You can identify me in a lot of ways, like "a weird guy" or "a cool dude" or just "the narrator" who tells the reader all about this book. Either way, I'm not offended if I'm identified as a joke. Everyone has his or her opinion; no one in the world would have the same positive opinion about someone; nor would anyone have the same negative opinion about someone. Unless the opinion is about rodents—but they aren't human. Just kidding, some people love rodents.

15

DEFINING A TIGER

One evening, I was eating dinner in a fancy restaurant with my mom, Mormor, Uncle Ken, and Aunt Renee. We were asking each other questions like: "Where is the one place in the world that you would like to go?" Then Aunt Renee asked, "What animal would you like to be if you were one?" I replied by saying that I would be a tiger. I said that just because "Tiger" sounded a little like my name. After dinner, I began to write reasons why I chose the tiger.

This was the only "free" chapter that I shared with hundreds of people. I shared my reasons for choosing a tiger with my writing class, my family, and my friends. I started out the story by saying, "Hey, kids! It's your old pal and friend. Do you have a favorite animal? I have a favorite animal too. It is the tiger. Here in this group of words, I will tell you why I like the tiger and compare my reasons why I like the tiger to real life events." Then I read the following:

Tigers are brightly colored cats with black stripes. Their color of fur is bright orange, but covering that orange is the dark black stripes. I have bright moments, but sometimes they cloud up with dark moments. Those stripes allow the tiger to blend in with certain surroundings that will make the tiger camouflaged so it can hide. A balance of good moods and bad moods makes it easy to blend into "normal." If a tiger would be nothing but black, then everyone would know where the "black" tiger would be. Plus, then it would be a panther, and panthers are good at hunting at night. If it were to be all orange, then it would be a cougar. No need to brag, but I'm the best at hide-and-go-seek. Quietly and patiently I hide and make myself comfortable in the forest.

The claws are meant to grab and hold onto their prey. I can grab a hold of something when it comes to goals, and not let go until it's done.

An average tiger can run fifty miles an hour. I can't run fifty, but I sure can run fast. Naturally, a person can run fast; my record is twenty miles an hour. Tigers, however, can't outrun a cheetah since they go an average of seventy miles an hour. I am not the fastest person in the world, but it sure is fun feeling that wind. No one can run without powerful legs.

When I see the eyes, they are focused and calm. Even though the tiger is one of the deadliest animals on the planet, it still has calm eyes. When there's trouble going on at school like a threat toward me, I don't shiver. I know they can't do such things to me. I may look calm, but I have full control of myself and follow my ways of life.

When I see the teeth, I see that they are powerful and bring out fear in others. At times, I've had moments where I literally scare people from my own actions. Sometimes, I don't mean to, but I do a lot of times; I never worry about what I do because I'm me. I don't see the tigers' teeth very often unless they are yawning.

The snarl of a tiger makes others stand aside. I never liked it when people wanted me to change, so I say "back off" or anything to make them leave me alone. I hate change in me. Except if it's on the outside like a haircut or new clothes.

The tiger's ears are meant for hearing prey coming close by. I like to multitask by listening to one thing, and then go to the other. Whenever I think I might hear something, I silence everyone and hear the sound. Tigers would hear another animal whether or not it was a good animal. I listen to people whether they are good people to be with or not.

Same thing with the nose; if a tiger smells something nice, he eats it. If not, he leaves it alone. If people have personalities that stink, I walk away.

When I looked at the lifespan of a tiger, I found out that they live about fifteen years. When my lifespan as a child ended at age fifteen, I felt dead inside. My teenage acquaintances can't be as active as they were when they were little kids. I am always ready for almost anything because I hate boredom and am always active except for bedtime. I act my age; it's just that people my age are not as active as they were a long time ago. I still don't understand that, but anyone can be as active as a child the way I see it. Any animal and any human can live longer than what their average is. At age fifteen, it seemed like my childhood was dying. I wish I could be a child again with my acquaintances as if I were back in the '90s. My childhood I will keep forever, no matter how many people grow out of it.

Every animal has its senses. Most even have tails. Sometimes, we can all relate to our favorite animals. Go on, pick an animal that you like, and explain why you chose it.

Since I wrote this essay, I've encouraged others to write about their favorite animals and why they like them. People sure make wonderful stories out of their animals.

16

MISSED OUT DECADES

I feel sometimes like I grew up in every decade while I've been alive. I lived through most of the '90s when I was very little, and then it came to the doubles zeros (00s) and the '10s, and yes I'm talking about the 2010s. That's the thing about decades; now we are in the 2010s era. We will get mixed up in the future on what decade is which. Is it the 1930s or the 2030s?

People think that kids would stick to what they know and what's going on right in the present and not be open to the past. Most of the time, that seems boring. I like to think of the present, but even with the past, there are still chances to experience what has already been experienced. I spread out to what I didn't get a chance to live through.

These missed out decades make me wonder why they can't be in the present that we are in now. The '50s had great food, waitresses on roller skates, drive-in movie theaters, and trays that were put on the car's window. I loved their leather jackets and their hairstyles back in the day. It seemed as though life was easy and everyone had fun. Of course, like I said, no one has had a completely fun life during his or her lifespan. Everyone makes mistakes. In the 1950s, it looked as if things were a lot smoother and people really knew how to have fun. The music was awesome too. They used record players instead of MP3 players. They discovered The King of Rock 'n' Roll: Elvis Presley. That dude was amazing! He was like the first coolest guy of rock 'n' roll. I love listening to his songs and looking at his style of clothing. To me, he was the icon of the 1950s. Although, and I would like to get it out of my mind, I didn't like how they treated people of different races back then; that's the only thing I don't like about that decade. Same with the '60s.

In the '60s and '70s, people were very creative in a lot of ways. The funny part is that there were hippies who were stoked up on smoking and wanted peace in the world. I'm not for the war, or peace. In other words, I don't take sides. Anyway, I liked the music in those decades. The styles of clothing and hair were really stylish. My mom and dad grew up in the '70s and said it was great growing up during those years. The schools were really balanced between having fun and being serious at the same time. It stinks that disco is dead because that's one of my favorite genres of music. In my mind, I don't really think that "Disco's dead" because if it were dead, no one would think about it or even listen to it ever again. Think about it, friends. Come to think of it, I would be a great disco king if I had the clothes. That would be cool. If I were to get a souvenir from the '70s, I would get that Volkswagen Samba Bus.

Music, movies, clothing, hairstyles, and dancing have never been better than they were in the '80s. It's the decade I like the most next to the '90s. The '80s were, I guess, the "old times" people talk about. My mom and dad will say, "just like old times." If I were to see an all out '80s dude, I'd see Bruce and Ken Tindall, my uncles on my mom's side of the family. Everything I see in them is '80s—memories, looks, music they play, and cars. I got so into the '80s that I wanted to dress like a party dancer from the '80s. I wore a tie around my head, had my hair spiked up to the side, wore a light brown buttoned up shirt with a white T-shirt inside and tucked in, worn out jeans, and torn shoes. I was a real party dancer and danced like I had never danced before. During spirit week in school, we had to wear certain things each day. One day was a decade day, so I dressed up as an '80s party dancer.

I'm glad I lived most of my childhood years in the '90s. I can still remember the music back then. The '90s were amazing. It was like the year of the street. We would have music and cool people back then. I was too young to go all street urban wise, but I admired everything street people were in the '90s. I remember the old Nintendo 64. Still the best video game console I've ever had. It was back in the day when graphics were not that important, but just the fun of the game itself. I always thought that the N64 had amazing graphics because it's a video game. Nothing realistic, just terrific game play and awesome memories of having fun with my Dad. I am a fan of the old video games from the '70s, '80s, and '90s, including Pong. I like the new games too, but nothing can beat the classics. Graffiti in the city still looks awesome every time I see that kind of artwork. Then I learned that it's illegal. Sorry artists. Not a lot of people can read graffiti writing, so I help them with what they said on the walls. As a joke, I say, "Take it from me; I'm from Portland" because there's a lot of urban artwork over there too. I was born in Portland, by the way. The '90s wasn't much of a missed out decade: 1994 was a good year to start living.

All of these decades were great; I've always wanted to live through every single one of them. In the '00s, everything was modernized and relied on digital technology. Everything now is done on computers. I used a computer typing this, but I handwrite in my spare time in school and other places. To be honest, I like using the computer and it's still really cool. I always wonder what would happen to this world if computers and fancy cell phones were to disappear. Would it make everything change back to the way things were in earlier decades? Or would people overreact and be lost about what to do afterwards? Welcome to the digital age.

17
GROWTH OF THE INVISIBLE BOY

I guess you could say that I am visible to the real world, which is outside school. Just joking; school is part of the real world. Whenever I'm in school, I become this person who is never noticed by my peers. My peers, I tell you. Almost every time I sit at a lunch table, I am not noticed. Even if I am noticed, people will only ask me whether they can sit in my spot. I stand up and walk away since I'm a nice guy. Still, it doesn't feel good to have them ask me to move.

I still don't understand why I get rejected like that. I am still human, I have good looks, I like to write, I am very active, I do a lot of things that are cool. Yet I am rejected. I guess I was right when I said, "I am my own self." Maybe people don't want to be themselves and a part of others. That's what I was saying when I was talking about worlds in the first chapter. Worlds choose to become populations when they collide with one another. That's the way I see it.

In my junior year, I met these two new kids who were from different countries. One from Germany and one from Turkey. When I saw those two sitting alone in the cafeteria, I decided to go over to them and play cards. They thought it was cool for someone to bring cards to school. We played Speed, Crazy

Eights, and Kings Corners. The girl from Turkey was more into cards than the German boy. He seemed sad and quiet. It is understandable that he missed his country and his family there. He said that he loves to cook and bake with his parents. For me, we were the three invisible people of the cafeteria, and we made a good team. We also had the same American Studies class so we sat together.

The two of them liked to pass notes to each other because they got bored really easily during American Studies. I was very surprised with their writing. When I passed notes to them, they wrote as if they were on a computer chat with the smiley faces and such. I thought it was funny and kept the conversation going while listening to the teacher. I'm good at multitasking so I take notes, play solitaire, talk to the cool foreign kids, and listen to the teacher. I tried talking to the German fellow, but it always seemed like he had a lot on his mind. I thought it might be personal, so I let him be. I always tried to cheer him up by saying, "Hi" to him every day and inviting him to a note chat. When I learned that he was leaving after the first semester, I felt very sad. I wanted to know him better. He seemed like a cool guy, but I understood that he had to go home to Germany and see his family. That part I was happy for. At least I had the Turkish girl since she stayed for the whole year.

One big reason why I titled this chapter "Growth of the Invisible Boy" is because as I grow, I become more invisible than I was before. Back when I was six years old in elementary school, teachers would put me in the "cloak of invisibility." It was all pretend since I'm not supposed to be in the teacher's lounge unless it's for something important. When I went to school with my peers then, I felt rejected too. Not as rejected as in high school, but I do feel like that "cloak of invisibility" is working pretty well.

I wanted to bring back my fellow classmates from elementary school. It seemed as though when they grew older, they turned from good guys into bad guys, acting spoiled and thinking they could do whatever they wanted and get whatever they wanted. I kept my spirit the same from the start of elementary school, and I was happy with everything I had, and I still am. I never wanted to change, but I do want my classmates from elementary school to understand me. It seems impossible since I'm a growing invisi-ble...thing. I am not noticed, and I will become entirely invisible by the time school ends. All ghosts are "bad" and are never to be treated as "friendly" ghosts. Saying that, I try everything I can to get my classmates' attention. I even told lies, saying I don't have a family and live on a boat. The reason behind that lie can be translated as: "I don't have a family that is like yours, and I'm happy for what I have; I'm not as spoiled as you." Still, it wasn't the best thing to do. Originally, I was going to call this chapter "Growing Ghost." But ghosts are bad, and I'm not bad. So, in-visible sounds better, even though it has more syllables and more words as a chapter title.

I may try to keep getting back my elementary school class-mates, but I still have the best friends in Gig Harbor where Dad is. I also have those cool kids from Turkey and Germany. After thinking that through, I began having thoughts about an epic battle with a title like: "Tyler's Friends vs. Elementary School Acquaintances." Tyler's friends will always win and force the oth-er team to join Tyler's friends and give Tyler respect.

If you are reading this book, my longtime fellow acquaintanc-es from Wilkes Elementary, we have known each other's names, we see each other a lot, but we have never ever met each other. I would be honored to take the time to shake your hand and get to know you all much better. Thank you for reading this chapter.

18

RUNNING WITH THE WIND

I overheard some people saying that a certain person was the fastest in the school. I asked them, "Does he run with the wind?" They answered, saying, "Well, he runs like the wind." then I said, "Then he's alone while running."

Even people who run would run with someone. The wind will always be with the runner wherever he or she goes. You feel it, you hear it, you breathe it. A runner is a living object of the world. The wind is like the giver of life. When the runner runs, he/she gets the wind and life will come to him/her. They say that life is a journey, not a destination. People don't have to be runners to get a hold of the "wind." Experiencing life is like running. Having fun makes the runner go faster and feel free.

I have been a runner since I was a little dude. I liked to run away from my parents and hide somewhere in the store or anywhere. I was a troublesome little boy, and I got in trouble almost every time. I view it as the more you're in trouble in your childhood, the more freedom you will soon have in the future after learning from that experience.

My favorite running memories were during recess when I was in elementary school. I would run with my former classmates and we would have a great time sharing the wind with each other. Now, it's not the same in high school. But I'm never alone when I'm running with the wind.

Then I overheard people saying that this person was faster than me. I asked, "Does he run in the rain?" they answered, "No, he doesn't; what's the point?" Then I said, "Then he's not a real runner if he can't run in any condition, including rain."

I live close to the school—about five football fields away. I would run to school every day, and run back home. That's when I had to carry a heavy backpack with me. It's funny; I can still run fast with a backpack, but when I take it off, I'm much faster. That's why I did track for two years.

Running in track was an amazing experience. There was this one time when I was in the bus and there were some kids who wanted to do the Ironman Challenge. I had no idea what the Ironman Challenge was. Then when I learned about the Ironman Challenge, I decided to accept it for the first time! The Ironman Challenge is a hard challenge where runners have to do every track event on one day. So that means hurdles, dashes, long distances, everything track-wise. First place is optional for each challenge. It was such an awesome experience that I even got an award for "most inspirational." I keep that treasure in my room. I also won some races—the 100 meters and 200 meters. I'm a sprinter.

Just to let you know, I'm not the fastest runner in the world. I try to be, but it hurts.

19

BROKEN CITY

It is easy to understand that we as humans are broken at some point in time. That never means that it's the time to give up. I've broken my collarbone, my right leg, and my right ring finger, and I still run like everyone else.

Yet, every time I look at my bent finger, it is always a bad luck symbol. I can even feel that bent feeling on my finger. It hurts to look at it, but I can't slow down to a finger.

When I look around Seattle, I see lots of homeless people wanting change or food. I always wonder why they are homeless and out in the streets; I figure that if they want money, they could go out and get some by asking for a job in a snap. I guess things are a lot more complicated when you're older and it comes to being homeless in my opinion. I always thought things would be very simple.

Like when we are at war, why can't the general say, "Stop fighting us!" and the other general would say, "Why? Are you a coward?" Then they would argue, saying, "I have this reason for fighting you; what's yours?" "This is my reason for fighting you." "Is it really all that important? Why can't we stop?" "I don't know; a lot of people have been killed during battle, and that is very sad." "Well, I don't want another soldier dying; let's stop the war and be friends." "Yeah, that's a great idea." Then the war ends. Sadly, it doesn't work that way.

Cities get old, and I can see hidden cracks on the roads and buildings. They remind me of people sometimes. They form cracks or troubles in their lives. I have a ton of cracks in me. Meaning that I have made a lot of trouble over the years, but I learned from my mistakes and moved on like the cracks weren't even there. But, when the cracks get huge, they need to go away before more trouble comes. So people clear up the big cracks.

A lot of history goes into a city. Throughout history, generation after generation, cities grow, have more experiences, and create more memories for their residents. Same with people; experience is worth having the rusty old cracks or damaged stuff. Albert Einstein said, "A person who never made a mistake never tried anything new."

Sometimes, I like to remember the mistake for a long time and then learn how it got fixed. Mistakes are great for a lot of things—as long as I learn from them, they are still an experience worth trying. If I were to be drinking, taking drugs, and all that stuff that the police would not like, then it would be a "trapped experience." When I go into the trap, there is no turning back. Here is my advice: "Kids, don't fight the law, and listen to your parents." Don't have a crack in your city so large it swallows up cars." That's why a lot of people, including your parents, say, "It's all your fault!" Especially when you're doing something bad.

20

WORLDS' ORBITS

The orbit of a world is simple. It goes around the sun. The sun represents personality. Now check this out below. It's about your personality towards others and yourself.

What is your personality? Please be honest and explain:

_____

_____

_____

Now, if you have a personality where you are hard on others and on yourself, then you are closer to the sun. The sun can harden planets when they are close to the sun. If you have a soft personality where you are calm and careful with yourself and with others, then you are farther from the sun.

Now the sun is just a star, so that means that throughout the galaxy, there are other stars that are just like the sun. There's lots and lots of suns, I should say.

Sun = City

Now, the reason why I said that the sun equals a city is because after being in cities for a while, I've learned that there are many people who react similarly with each other. Take, for example, Seattle. A lot of people are down mostly because of the rain, but that doesn't mean that everyone is down all the time over there. Now we have an orbit of "Seattle's personality" over there. We go around the sun around to the left, around to the right, over, under, and any other ways you can think of.

Now if a world wants to go somewhere else in the galaxy, it will always be warm with personality because it is the sun that makes the planets keep their texture. So in other words, we keep our personality no matter where we go.

A supernova is a death of a star. Our sun can never die, but since we are worlds that are also stars, we explode. It really is a tragic thing to see and a supernova effects other worlds around the galaxy—especially those who love you and care about you very much.

Supernova = Death

There is nothing super about it.

There are so many people who view life in different ways. Personally, I view it astronomically in space because space itself is full of life. The orbit of planets and stars is what keeps the universe moving. It keeps it alive.

21

THE SENIOR FAREWELL

Recently, I was thinking about the news article I wrote in the school newspaper when I was a freshman to all the seniors who graduated. The seniors of 2009 were special and I wanted to let them know how much I'm going to miss them. Here is the article I wrote:

GOODBYE SENIORS!
TYLER MCNAMER
GUEST REPORTER

"I can't believe it! The big kids are going away!" That's what I would say if I were in first grade, but I'm not in first grade anymore—I'm just a freshman. But since you're reading this, I'll say it again: "I can't believe it! The big kids are going away!"

Every time I walk to school, every time I sit in my classes, at lunch, on the grass, or even by your side, I always feel happy with all the people who make this school a whole unit, and that includes the senior students. For the most part, every grade is separated into its own place during lunches. While kids don't feel like they have to be in the same place every day, they go to the table or place because their closest friends are sitting there. My fellow freshman classmates and I feel like we have a lot of freedom, but you seniors, you get to do almost anything in the world.

I think every freshman should take the opportunity to get to know all of you. Every one of you is the icon for the whole island and your full blooded Spartan spirit; the true high school spirit that has the power of cheering for your friends and having fun with them! As seniors, you have set the example for the underclassmen on campus. To those who still haven't learned this, they are missing out on your wiseness. Well, anyway, I just wish my fellow freshman friends would know the ways of the Spartan Spirit like you guys. I always love it when you guys cheer us Spartans on. One person yells "Go!" and a huge wave of fans cheer "SPARTANS!!!!!!" The shouts are those of freshmen, juniors, and sophomores, but the ones who start the Spartan Spirit roar are the seniors!

It's close to summer, and I bet you're all excited and looking forward to fun in the sun and then going off to college in the fall. I'm excited for you too! But I am also sad to see all of you go. All of you bring a smile to my face by making the school complete. When I go back to school after summer vacation, it may not be the same without you. Not that I don't trust the juniors and sophomores, but you know what I mean.

So before you guys go, I'm writing this to thank you for opening my heart to school, and I'll just say this one last thing—Goodbye Seniors, and good luck in finding your future!

If you are reading this again, my former senior friends, I hope you all are doing great. I usually say, "Go Spartans" at the games, but since you're all moving on with your awesome lives,

I'll sum it up with two of the same words. GO SPARTANS! As a matter of fact, it never was the same without the "original" seniors from when I was a freshman. Everyone was good, but not as good as the class of 2009. I guess it's fun being the one standing up and being next to the big people.

22

SECRET DOWNERS

Every time I walk to school, I see other kids with different facial expressions as they walk to school or to a different class. Almost everyone I see looks down at the ground. It always tells me that things have not been going very well in their worlds. So I ask most of them, "What's wrong?" They respond with, "Nothing." So I say, "Okay, I'm sure you will be good tomorrow."

The next day, I see the same people with the same looks on their faces. When I ask what's wrong, they say, "Nothing." So I say, "It's been tomorrow; you haven't changed since yesterday; is something up?" The person might then reply, "I need my space; you're not an adult to speak with." Then I walk away without another word.

I understand when people say I'm not an adult. So I leave a lot of people alone when they deserve it. I always want to help my peers, but I guess I'm too young to do that. Plus, people will wonder how someone who has autism could have the ability to help people. Well, I'm like everyone else, but I view the world differently.

Every day after school, the kids will go to the only place to hang out. Safeway. It sounds ridiculous, but it's true; most of the kids will go to Safeway just to hang out. I always thought it was crazy and hoped that someday we would have a bowling alley. When I see the kids going down to Safeway, I still see most of them looking down as they walk, but I guess they "have no choice" but to hang out over there, or even something else going on in their lives. Relationship problems? Family issues? Boredom? It's none of my business, but I do like to figure out sometimes what's going on with people.

Even the parents have their down looks when picking up their kids. Even if I were to wave to them, they wouldn't respond. Sometimes, I ask myself the same questions: Relationship problems? Family issues? Boredom? I guess no one is too old or too young for asking those questions.

Sometimes, I wonder whether parents today really care about and love their child or children. Almost everywhere I turn, there's always someone who says or does the stupidest things. I ask the three questions again: Relationship problems? Family issues? Boredom? From where I was in high school, most of the things everyone talked about were the times they had with each other, whether it was dating, or looking forward to being a frat boy or girl. To me, it's somewhat part of the boredom area. I'm not saying that's a bad thing; it's just the way I see it. There are other questions besides those three; I just give those as examples. There are many questions for people who are down, and maybe you can think of some that I haven't thought of yet.

Every time I go to school, I make sure I release my feelings through the way I walk or sit down. Like when I'm happy, I walk joyfully and whistle a tune. I'm not afraid to do that. But I don't want to show my feelings when it comes to angry moments. Anger is not really the best way to go, and I take it out by exercising or fighting my shadow. Except that unexpected time at the assembly that I mentioned in Chapter 5. I'm not perfect, but sometimes I have had those moments. It is not right when I let anger get the better of me.

Maybe people are down by the way they look every day. I know I was, and I understand how they feel. Not everyone is very confident about how he or she looks. Not even the male and female supermodels are all that confident. For example, the beautiful Marilyn Monroe. She was titled "The sexiest girl in the world." She had moments that sparkled Hollywood and the planet. But you know how she died? She took a drug overdose and died because of it. Her beauty still touches our hearts today, and it's a shame that she did not live on. If she were still alive, she would see people making movies about Marilyn Monroe starring Marilyn Monroe!

Another famous person is the King of Rock 'n' Roll, Elvis Presley. He was known as the king because he was the greatest performer in rock 'n' roll history. He had everything: fame, money, hairstyle, looks, voice—everything! You know how he died? Drug overdose! The drugs ended his life, but he will always be in our hearts forever. Don't ever forget about the King of Rock 'n' Roll.

One last famous person is one of my favorite celebrities. The outgoing comedian Chris Farley! Chris had more than fame and money; he had fans and friends who loved him with their whole hearts, and he loved them back. Chris Farley did not like himself because of his weight. He became severely depressed and just wanted to end it all. So you know what he did? You guessed it—he overdosed on drugs. His friends missed him, his celebrity friends miss him, his fans miss him, I miss him.

These three famous people had a love for what they did and who they were as people. Yet drugs took over their lives and killed them all. It almost seems as if the iconic people die young; that is why I choose not to take drugs. I take the examples of the once living icons who are now dead; drugs killed the most beloved of them. Don't let that happen to you.

There are kids who are happy when they are with friends, but when they aren't around their friends, they have their down faces. I always wonder, "Who are they for real? Up people or down people?"

I always thought that no matter how old you are, you can still help others. I almost made my own psychiatric stand for people to come in and tell me their problems like in the *Peanuts* comics where Lucy has her "Psychiatric Help" stand to help Charlie Brown and learn what's in his thoughts. I didn't put the stand up because you have to be licensed to be a psychiatrist. So I thought I better wait until I'm older so I can ask people what troubles them.

I think people can be blind even when being successful and cool. Even lost for that matter. I get blind sometimes. But I find myself a lot of times. It makes me a happy person whenever I find myself. Then when people ask me, "What's up?" I say, "I'm up."

23

THE EFFORTLESS

I was watching this awesome music video from VH1 classics. A lot of music videos are sweet, but this one, in my opinion, showed real talent. It was, "Take On Me" by A-ha. The animation, the music, the storyline, and the people in it were all amazing.

I bet you are wondering why the title of this chapter is called "The Effortless." Well, my fellow readers, as I grow up in the 2010s, I see quite a few people who get paid for having hardly any talent whatsoever. I cannot tell you who is on the no talent list; I'll leave it up to you to figure out who is part of "the effortless."

I am surprised that people admire the effortless even more than the ones who put a lot of effort into what they do. Now, just know, I'm not trying to change people's likes or dislikes; I just like to point out the things I see. No one can judge that.

When I started to notice the effortless, I began to make it a big deal in my head. I questioned the effortless in my mind. Then I came up with answers in my brain. Perhaps people like the effortless because they like to see them for "who they are." Well, sure, but they are just like the other people who are around them who aren't on TV. Perhaps people like the talentless because they themselves have no talent and thought that the talentless were better than them. So that's entertaining for them. Perhaps boredom is the new talent. Or perhaps as time goes on, people won't have great talented minds like people did years earlier.

Anything can be an answer; there is no such thing as a true answer when it comes to stuff like this. I like watching the effortless who do not require a screen. Watching the effortless is for free in the real world. Maybe, just maybe...the (talentless) will be talented in a way that will soon affect the world for real—whether it's showing courage to do something great like becoming the next generation artist or a stand-up comedian who would spread the humor to the world. Everyone has a talent and just needs to have the courage to realize it. My talent is...well, come to think of it, I shouldn't say, "Everyone has a talent because then it would be one lonely thing that would be released". I think there are many wonderful talents that people have, and they can all show them off with courage and strength. Go on, my friend; what are your greatest talents? Do you have in you the effort to make them come true?

24

SCHOOL STORIES

In the movies, one character often becomes the most important person in high school. His story or her story can be that of someone who is "popular" or an "underdog." This person makes high school look like fun by the way he or she acts in the movies, but in real life, anyone can make high school or even school itself fun by the choices he or she makes.

Not a lot of kids in my school are interesting, whether they are underdogs or not. In fact, I don't really see any "popular" kids in my school. I guess the "popular" kids thing is just a myth in my opinion.

I would look at a person; then I would "switch eyes" with him so I could see what he could see, and what it's like to be him for ten seconds. It turns out that even then the person is still a mystery. Even if I were to "switch eyes," I would see what he sees, but I don't think like him. It's like a first person switch.

As I would read books and watch movies about high school, I came to the point where I asked, "Shouldn't the teachers have their stories too?" I thought that since teachers are in school, and they teach children good things, teachers should be main characters. I bet there are main characters who are teachers, but I haven't read those books or seen the movies yet.

Whenever I look at someone, I feel like that person has a story of his own. When there is a happy person, then his story is happy. When there is a sad person, then his story is sad. When there is a mad person... well, you get the idea.

When I was little, I would love to listen to stories about a lot of things like fairy tales and nursery rhymes. Today, I view "scary tales" and "nursery crimes" in the real world. Scary crimes or nursery tales or not, they are full of action and adventure, sometimes thrilling and sometimes frightening.

When I was in intermediate school, I would want to start a conversation with different peers just to hear their stories. Everyone I asked about his or her story would say, "I've got no story to share with you." But I always thought that when it comes to conversations, people are sharing their stories. Hearing what they said, though, sounded like a bunch of boring stories to me. Even in high school, stories never interest me when they come from people my age. But at least they are stories.

In elementary school, I was one of the characters in everyone's story. Everyone who became my acquaintance, that is. It seems as if my acquaintances don't like to tell their school stories now. I remember what some of their story plots were because I was in them. To me, it's always important to remember the past; that way, I have a keen sense of memory when it comes to the present and the future. To me, it felt like a great story to tell because of the experience and excitement. I know it doesn't entertain everyone else, but it's good to tell the story to myself.

Some kids will tell stories just to be dramatic and be noticed. In response, I think, "Oh, please, there is no one to blame but yourself." When it comes to stories, they can be entertaining and ridiculous at the same time. No one can make a person dramatic;

that's impossible unless you're in drama class, but it can't be dramatic all the time. It's fun to see it in a theater, but not anywhere else.

School stories are exciting because they are all about discovery and creativity. By creativity, I mean the way the main character goes through school. Does he/she do it in a fun way? A boring way? A depressing way? Anything can happen with creativity and experience. Most stories don't include school, but to me, school stories are really cool. What's your school story?

25

THE RAINBOW SEED

I learned how to read before I talked. I learned how to write before learning how to sit on a chair. It seems funny because when I was a toddler, I had trouble sitting still. So I would write in a notebook sometimes. When I was in third grade, we had a homework assignment saying that we had to come up with a story about flowers. Unlike most of the boys in my school, I happened to like flowers a lot. I would give flowers to people and keep some for myself. So I got excited to write something about flowers. When I was little, my favorite color was "rainbow" because it had all the main colors. Then when I was in sixth grade, I learned that rainbow is not a color, so I changed it to red.

Following is basically my first published story. I was given great thanks by my parents, teachers, and long lost friends at school for this cool story. I did my best to remember every moment of the story since I don't have it with me while writing this book.

THE RAINBOW SEED
BY TYLER MCNAMER

On a faraway farm, there lived a little boy named Ted. Friends called him Teddy for his nickname. He lived in an old broken home with his mom, Susie, in the middle of nowhere. They couldn't see any flowers surrounding them—nothing but dry land and a roadway to the store.

Then one day, Teddy decided to walk around the mountains with his friends when he met an old man. "Hello, young boy!" said the man. "I am Old Man Harry. I want to do something good for you and your mom." Then Harry brought forth a beautiful brightly colored seed that changed color over time. "What is it?" asked the boy. "It's a Rainbow Seed. I want you to plant it," replied the jolly old man. The boy Teddy had never planted a seed before, so Harry took him down from the mountains and showed him how to plant a seed. "You see, young fellow, you place the seed in the ground; you water it once in awhile, make sure the sun shines down on the seed, and let it grow over time." So Old Man Harry gave Ted the rainbow seed and left with a warning, saying, "Remember, boy; this seed is gifted; you will be up for a big surprise," and off he went into the distance.

Teddy rushed home to tell his mom about what had happened and she got excited about the seed. They both went outside right at the back side of the house and planted the colorful seed.

Then all of a sudden, the seed grew a huge rainbow and stretched far over the fields. It was a hot and sunny day, so the sun melted the rainbow slowly. With the rainbow melting, the droplets from the rainbow turned into little seeds and went straight to the ground. With that, the seeds quickly turned into rainbow flowers. They had different colors of flowers everywhere all over the fields.

Teddy and his mom, Susie, were so happy to see all that happening to their field, and they began to smell the scent of the flowers all over. People all over got to see the flowers, and everything was just amazing for the boy and his mom, all thanks to a little seed that needed to be planted.

The End

After remembering most of the aspects of that story I made up, I started to wonder what was the purpose of writing it. Everything has a purpose. One of the things that I've learned after re-reading this story was that it takes just one seed to become something beautiful. That beauty spreads, and it goes throughout a large area. Then later, the "flowers" are seen throughout the world by people, and when they are shown stories and pictures of the flowers, then they can all see them for real. I guess I can name this book you're reading a "rainbow seed" that might spread to other areas. Of course, there are people who are "allergic" to flowers, and that's all right; they don't have to be involved in the "seed" known as *Population: One*.

Another thing I've noticed is that my story sounds a little like Dr. Seuss' *The Lorax*, but when I was little, I never read that book. I was still reading the simpler books by Dr. Seuss. The similarity is in the part where the trees are flowers, and the two stories didn't have any plants to begin with. Except *The Lorax* story once had trees. My story did not have any plants to begin with. After reading *The Lorax*, I thought it must have been a coincidence to write that when I was little and didn't know *The Lorax* in the first place. I'm always that kind of boy who never wants to take ideas from someone else, so like I said before, it must have been a coincidence.

It just takes one tiny seed to make something big and beautiful. That's what that story was about. Do you have a rainbow seed?

26

MEDIA MENTORS

The plot is simple; there is a tall, dark, and handsome young man who has all the charm. Then there is a short, not-so-good-looking boy who doesn't have a lot of charm. Then there is a beautiful girl who is sweet and kind. The not-so-good-looking boy has a crush on the beautiful girl, and so does the handsome young man. In the end, the not-so-good-looking boy gets the girl of his dreams. As for the handsome young man, he was the bad guy in the whole plot.

If there is one thing I've learned about a plot similar to this one in the movies, it's that girls in my high school are into the "ugly." Well, maybe I shouldn't say that, but I have seen quite a lot of not-so-good-looking people who are strangely attractive to others.

Now, I already know that saying, "Don't judge a book by its cover." I understand that. The way I see it, if the book is called *The Ugly Fat Girl*, I don't need to read it. You see, my dear readers, don't take it the wrong way; I care about people on the inside *and* the outside. If people take care of themselves on the outside, then they love themselves. That makes them attractive to others. But, here is the biggest "but" of all—if people can't help having a sickness that causes "outside ugliness," then it's all about the inside. In my opinion, plastic surgery makes people look even worse. Like I said before, I'm never afraid of sharing my thoughts with the world. It's always good just to get them out. Sometimes, I feel silly saying these things, but in the end, I'm proud I did.

Now back to this chapter's theme; a lot of movies have action scenes, and people in real life like to reenact these awesome acts. It's not wrong to reenact the stunts, but it's dangerous.

Then, there are times when people at a young age want to join the army. In my opinion, this desire comes from war movies and video games. I'm not saying that those games or movies should be banned; I just think they have that kind of influence. If I were to be in an army, I would use paintball and air softener guns. I never really saw paintball movies or air softener movies before. With gun movies, it's all about the bloody deaths.

At the end of almost every movie, the good guy wins, the bad guy loses. Big surprise, right? The way I see it is that the bad guy would have the best scenes in the movie before he is defeated. That's why most people like the bad guys as their favorite characters. The good guys usually save the day, but people want to know how they save the day, and for them to do it in an exciting way.

In romantic movies, lovers are made to look like they are going to love each other forever and ever. But the sad truth is, that's never the case in real life. I remember seeing one girl, who was a stranger I happened to see at a park, who had a tattoo that said "Love Never Dies!" I took a long look at it and secretly laughed in my head. Tattoos wear out over time. I bet that tattoo will end up saying: "Lve er es!"

27

MY VIEW OF LOVE

You kids probably see boyfriends and girlfriends during your school day. Some of you readers are in a relationship. Now hear me out because I'll tell you how I view love.

There are many types of "love" that affect everyone:

- Dark Love - People love scary stuff and are meant to have scary looks like Goths.
- Celebrity Love - I have that type too. I've got my heart set on Chris Farley.
- Ego Love - "I'm the best! All must respect me!" Sadly people *love* having that.
- Pornographic Love - I'm not going to explain that.
- Violent Love - War machines who love the thrill of violence, like hardcore gamers.
- Social Love - It's a great way to be friends with people for those who love to socialize.
- Isolation Love - The corner is a best friend to those who have this type.

The list goes on and on. It is all part of this world.

Whenever I see kids who have boyfriends or girlfriends, I see how they get along. They get along great at first; then a few months later, things don't turn out great. It almost seems as if "love" changes people—especially when they are in high school.

When I was in elementary school, I "loved" to play. It was fun to play with others as well—boy, girl, or teacher. I was a playful little dude. I didn't need to talk much in order to play. I felt loved by everyone because I was a fun guy. I still am, you know, but as time goes on, it seemed like people felt that "fun" was getting old. I mean, that's the way I saw it since there are not many people my current age who believe in recess in high school. Then again, I think there are—they are into "Playing in the Football Field." Then there is wintertime when the snow comes down. A secret rule came up that says, "When it's snowing, then it's play-time for everyone." Pretty cool secret rule, huh?

Like my mom and dad, I had to break many hearts. Dad broke Mom's; Mom broke those of lots of men who liked her. I had to do the same thing. I broke a lot of hearts. I did not believe in "having feelings" for someone. As a kid, breaking hearts is like routine for me. I never feel good at first, but it certainly gives me freedom.

I am a kid, a teen, so I have never had the time yet for adult acts. I'm saving my true love for someone gifted. Once I find her, then I'll probably write a love story called *Population: Two* But then comes the question: Who would want a boy like me? Well... only "other" people can and will decide on that.

Although, once there was someone I really adored and cared for. It was when I was in first through fourth grade. I loved her dearly. Then when my parents got separated, I was afraid to hurt her the same way they had hurt each other, so I purposely left her before anything serious went on within the heart. I was in tears because I hoped that I would never break her heart as the years went on.

Watching love movies makes it look like the lovers both are happy for each other. It makes me feel good looking at that. In real life in high school, it's a different story. I see most couples snuggle tightly together with hardly any words coming from them. I wonder to myself: "What are they scared of?" because that's what I would do to a stuffed animal when I'm scared of something. Besides moms and dads, boyfriends and girlfriends are people who only escape fear in my opinion. I think it's silly to date for a reason like that. Or is it?

Of course, everyone needs love in his or her life. I love the people who love me for who I am. My family, friends...and probably fans.

28

PICTURES AND SOUNDS

Many people learn better with pictures and sounds. Take me for a great example.

I love to read; reading takes a lot more creativity than watching a movie. I picture what's going on after reading one sentence. I will read it out loud, or in my head. But sometimes it's hard to get into the book because there are a lot of things going on. Personally, reading out loud is easy for me.

I've had classes where we had to read something and then explain what we had read. I'm good at explaining with the book. When the book is taken away, I lose the information I need to answer the questions.

With a book, there are a lot of words to remember. Picture books are easy to understand for most people. But then, sometimes, these books don't lead to good imagination because the pictures take away the imagination. I'm not saying that picture books are bad; I like picture books.

When I was little, I would go into my dad's office while he was on the phone. I didn't know that I was supposed to be quiet whenever he was on the phone. So Dad would take pictures of him making the "shush" pose when he was on the phone. He would tape them on the door so I could see it whenever the door closes. So that worked out great and I was quieter.

Sometimes, kids like to imitate what they see in paintings, movies, and other sorts of pictures like video games. But especially movies. As younger kids, we would imitate what adults said on TV, which would make us look weird. It was cool at first, but then it became an embarrassment to everyone, including me. But then when I do these embarrassing things, I become less ashamed of myself because over time, I get used to that feeling. So that's how I became a great leadership legend of BHS. It's not embarrassing when you're doing the appropriate things in life. Hopefully, people at school would picture me as a dude with great attitude.

Pictures don't have to be from a book; they can be from anything. They can include signs, movies, hands, eyes, and everything that's in anyone's sight. They are a great way to see something and be inspired by them.

Sounds are amazing. Sounds can affect people in so many different ways. They can be any sound like music, sound effects, voices, and so on.

I will be calm when there is calm music; I will be mad when there is mad music like heavy metal and such. I love all different kinds of music; it doesn't have to be the same genre all the time. To me, liking the same thing all the time makes it kind of boring. That's why when I was little, my favorite color was rainbow. Then I changed it to red.

In video games, I can hear the characters make sound effects to make the game cooler. Especially when it's a fighting game, I can hear them whenever they punch or kick. In real life, fighting is not as cool as it is in video games, which is why I try to avoid fighting as much as I can.

Speaking is another form of sound—the sound of words coming out of someone's mouth. They can affect everyone, bad or good. If people say good things all the time, it gets pretty boring and doesn't add character to anyone. If someone says, "Hey, I like your shirt" every time he/she sees you, it sounds too automatic and robotic. I mean, it's cool if that shirt is cool, 'cause I wear cool shirts every day (not really). But all I'm saying is that not every conversation is good; nor are they bad. The one thing I hate the most in the whole world is when someone lies. Most of us feel the same way about lies. In my opinion, if people were to be honest and say that my lips are too red, I would ask them why they thought so; then a whole conversation would begin. By the way, my lips are full of blood supply.

Music is amazing! Music is the best thing that's ever happened in the universe. Rock 'n' roll sooths the soul they say. They also say that disco is dead. To me, it lives on. If I were to have a theme song, I would choose...well, that's a tough one; I don't know really.

Sounds defy the planet, and so do pictures. Putting them together makes reality.

29

TRUE LEADERSHIP

This chapter is about leadership, and I know a lot about leadership. The reason why I know so much about leadership is because I'm usually the leader...got you, didn't I? This chapter may be called *True Leadership*, but to tell you the truth, not everyone will find true leadership because there are agreements and disagreements.

There are two different kinds of leadership. There is individual leadership, meaning that things happen all because of one individual. Then there is community leadership, meaning that great things happen to one another with teamwork. In high school, we lacked both individual and community leadership because everything out there was all done because of expectations—whether it was for assemblies, or for high school tolo dances, or for anything that was already planned out since I was a freshman, and even before that.

I discovered individual leadership myself when I wanted to make a change and a difference to the school dances. It was when I was a freshmen that I discovered leadership without being in a class.

Community leadership was not strong in school. I did not have a good time in leadership class; I was mostly in the corner shuffling cards, waiting for something new to happen and for me to help. No one, not even the ASB officers—members of the student government—came up to me to ask me to be a part of the group and work as a team; to me, they all seemed selfish. If I were the leader, I would think of the whole school rather than myself or those close to my side in the class. I knew that being an ASB officer requires lots of responsibility. To tell you the truth, I did not want that responsibility because I would save that responsibility for when I was older, not for being an ASB officer, but to get together with determined individuals who are willing to work together as a community to help one another and have fun.

Leadership requires teamwork and treating others how you want to be treated. It's a shame that not a lot of kids at my schools learned that. In my mind, that's how friendships evolve—by working together on anything. If it's something huge like being in a rock band or running a restaurant, that's when friendships occur and that makes friendships and their passion great.

I used individual leadership in writing this book. I made the decision to be a leader by writing this book, and now you're reading Chapter 29. Feels good doing it too.

To be honest, I think community leadership in kids is much stronger than it is when it comes to teenagers. To me, I think that no matter what a child has, whether the child is deaf, blind, or autistic, other kids would still accept that child for who he/she is, and when it comes to obstacle courses where you have to get to the other side with teamwork, I have seen kids working together as a team, and all of them make it together. Of course, not every kid is like that, but I think younger kids are more likely to have a strong community leadership than teenagers. As time goes on, kids go from community leadership, to individual leadership in the teenage years, and then back to community leadership in adulthood.

Then again, everyone is different when it comes to leadership. Some choose to have it, and others choose not to have it, not to be a leader of any kind.

Next to running and candy, leadership is a fun thing to have, and I think everyone should learn true leadership...led by me.

One other thing about leadership is how to avoid bad leadership. Treating other people badly is bad. Forcing others to do something is not good, and being egotistical about being the boss of everything is very bad. I showed ego in this as a joking matter—I was just having fun—and that's what leadership is all about. It's about having fun. Having fun with others who look up to you, and having fun with yourself doing things that affect those around you. All you have to do to get that leadership is to have the courage to make it happen. Take the passion and make it happen. Do not do it because you have to, but because you want to. To the men, I say, "You're the best!" To the women, I say, "You're the best!" Everyone can be equal, everyone is unique, and everyone can be a great leader.

30

"NOTHING" IS SOMETHING

Everyone does something with a purpose or a reason. There is no such thing as "nothing." The word "nothing" is something! It doesn't have to be anything, but it is something.

This "nothingness" is something because as soon as nothing starts, there is something else that happens after it. It doesn't have to make sense, but at least it's something.

Everyone and everything has something to say. Not just by speaking, but by showing itself. For example, a rock might say, "I'm a rock outside this house; you can sit on me if you like." The air says, "I will help you breathe. Just inhale me in and then exhale."

Now I will switch to another topic in this chapter that has a purpose. That's right—I'm talking about the word "purpose."

Well, it is almost the same thing as "Nothing is something." The word "purpose" is a very powerful word. When someone says that he doesn't have a purpose, that is a huge problem. A purpose to fail is a purpose all right, but I certainly don't like it. I guess the word "purpose" is another word for "something." Everyone has "something" to offer this world. But here is the big but. Not everyone will see that purpose for that someone. Everyone in the world will not know who I am, nor all of the other "well known" people alive today. Some people even think they don't have purpose, so they die young. Take for example Chris Farley. He had so many purposes in life, including making people laugh, but he ended his life anyway with a drug overdose.

The way I view it, the way to sum up the purpose of the word "purpose" is with a definition of "life." When people ask me what my purpose in life is, I respond by saying: "Life." There is no need for a complicated explanation; life is always an adventure, a journey. No matter how weird or unusual my actions were and are probably going to be in the future, it's all experience and time well spent. If you want to know your purpose in life, feel free to take my word for it and say "Life!"

Nothing IS something.

31

FIRST TIMERS

Everyone has had his first time with anything—same with me. I remember the first time I went to Mexico.

I felt that being a Caucasian tourist seemed pretty weird. It was great going to Mexico with Dad, but it did seem weird to me that we were the odd ones among all the Mexican people. In my head, I felt that we might ruin the culture of any country in the world. So I got nervous. But Dad says that countries and other places like Hawaii are expecting tourists like us. That did help me a bit, and I got used to being a tourist. It is always fun traveling places in the world.

Whenever I try something new that's physical, I tend to shake. I never mean to shake, but it just happens. Then after a while, I become a master at that physical thing, like with trap shooting or riding my bike.

All those new first time moments were easy to get used to. If there is one thing that is not easy to get used to, it is accepting my autism. It seems like I'm always a first-timer when it comes to that. Not all the time, though; I usually get the hang of accepting my autism, but it's hard because I am different from everyone else in the world.

A first time for other people, but not for me, is seeing the world the way I see it like my family members do. Yeah, I see the world differently; I even see the galaxy and the universe differently. It's never a bad thing to do because I will point out something, and then others can study what I point out. My family and friends get to have their first times studying what I think.

I love new things. Whenever I see something different, like tables set in a different way in class, I will say, "Oh, boy! A new thing is going on! I better go see!" I always have a hard time thinking stuff in my head instead of saying that stuff out loud. When it comes to new things like a school assembly, I get so excited because it's...well, it's something new and exciting. And because there is something going on that doesn't happen as often. A dancing contest for an opening assembly would make me so excited that my energy would be transferred into dancing.

Then there was my first time flying in a plane. It was a small plane owned by my dad's friend. He did the takeoffs and landings. When I was flying, I had no idea that going from Gig Harbor to Bainbridge would be that fast. I always wanted to skydive to school one day. Either that or I wanted to grab a hold of a ladder dropped from a helicopter, and ride the helicopter around the state of Washington. When I was up in the air, I thought how everyone looked so small. Just like when I'm on the ground, planes look so tiny when they are up in the air. Everything's bigger when you're right next to it.

Then there are first times that are not great; having my parents separated was not the best first experience in the world. During my first fight, I shook like I usually do in first time experiences. But then I went from being shaky to being active. I never ask for fights; they just usually happen in my life.

What about my first time writing a book? I'm as excited as ever! I'm so excited that I just want to end here and share it with the world. But I have much more to write. Stay gold, my readers.

32

EVIL IS ROUTINE

I've taken a good long look at how the world is defined. In my backyard, I see the grass. Simple and quiet. When I have left one of my two houses just to see a small chunk of the world, I have learned that evil is routine. Just to let you know, I'm not against anything or anyone. I say what I see.

At school, I have been in fights. I fight just for self-defense, but most people my age want to see a fight or be part of one. I don't like it.

In my school, a lot of "couples" fight as well; they argue and even beat up each other. I just walk by, minding my own business. Sometimes, they don't even look happy when they are together. Even pregnancy sometimes happens in high school. That makes me say, "Are you kidding me?"

One time after school, I went to Safeway to get my favorite candy bar, Snickers. I saw a ton of kids from high school coming to Safeway to hang out. I didn't think that was a bad thing until one day when my barber was cutting my hair, I asked him, "Why do kids go to Safeway to hang?" He replied, "There are a lot of thieves stealing food from Safeway. I guess it's their only place to hang out since there is nothing else to do for the high schoolers." Then I see kids smoking and looking like they always have hard times in their lives. Some even try to get away with doing drugs like cocaine and crack. I just hope someday when I'm all rich and what not, I can build a bowling alley with a restaurant, a snack bar, and an arcade.

Even just a small island like Bainbridge can have "issues" a lot of the time. It is like the world sometimes. Adultery is very common in the world. It's all about the sex everyone in the world likes. It's like a drug. Personally, I'll save it until I'm married. People all over pay for sex, sell for sex, kill for sex, take anyone for sex, and sacrifice for sex. There is probably more they do just for sex. Altogether, it counts as a natural, harmful, selfish drug.

Greed is very selfish. I never thought I would have to say anything that obvious. It's funny when people try to win in casinos. I remember this one time when a woman won $5,000 on a slot machine, and then guess what happened next? She spent it all on the same slot machine! How ridiculous was that? I didn't see it at the casino because I'm too young to be in one, but Dad told me all about it. I was playing this video game where you steal a car and hit a bunch of people and then take their money. Honestly, I thought it was funny in a sad way since it's on a video game, but a lot of people are like those video game characters. Not hitting them with cars, but stealing instead. I never played that game again. Yes, it is sad that people want more than they have already. In my opinion, I think they are afraid to become poor, so they will do anything to earn the bucks.

Natural disasters are very destructive and most countries have encountered them. It's no one's fault that there are earthquakes, tornadoes, floods, and all those horrific catastrophes. It's sad to say that they come naturally; it's normal to have bad weather like that. I do not like it one bit, but it is true.

Starvation is surprisingly high. I've seen skeletons with skin begging for life. I always wanted that to stop because I feel sad for them, and I feel how fortunate we are to have food. I am thankful that we have food, but I'm not thankful for learning about starving people in the world. Same thing with sickness; it's like a plague; it happens unexpectedly. Sickness can be small like a cold, and it can be large like AIDS. It's sad, but it is true.

Fights are good when I'm defending myself. My enemies are the attackers. In war, both sides are the attackers. Terrorists from the Middle East caused the epic horror of the Twin Towers crashing to the ground on September 11, 2001. Before I was born, my mom and dad went to the very top of the Twin Towers and said it was the most beautiful set of buildings in the world. I always wanted to go up there someday. But when I saw the plane crash on the news, my dreams of going up ended. I was mad for two days. After that, I just let it go. I didn't know how big and memorable that moment was until I was eleven. Yet, we are in war. My classmates in fifth grade said that "Everyone loves America." But that's not true. Like I said, no one in the world is going to like the same thing. Why are we still fighting? Why can't we stop the war in a snap? It's all about power. Nation against nation happens a lot in the world. When I see soldiers fighting, I don't see that they fight for their nations; they fight just to have a good hold on power. It is just like sex, but with power, and they would do anything to get power.

When I hear about death, I know that kids cry over their dead mom or dad. A family member will then go to the kids and say, "He/she is in a better place now." That part I hate the most. Why would the dead be in a "better place"? If I were to define a "better place" for the kids, I would say that parents being with their kids is much more important than anything else. If I were those kids, I would think, "Why would Mommy or Daddy be in a better place when they could be here with me?"

Sometimes people who want to be in this "better place" will even kill themselves just to see their dead family members once again.

You know it is very interesting when it comes to death because on December 14, 2012, there was the school shooting in Connecticut. I felt very sad to hear the news because kids, family members, and teachers should never go through anything so evil. Then I realized something. Everyone dies every day. Kids and adults die every day. So I then thought to myself, "Why is this such a big deal when there are so many people dying? It made me sick inside thinking about it. I've learned that death is nothing unique.

I could go on and on about this topic. The truth is, things in this world are not going well. But, that doesn't mean we have to stop living life and worry. I live my life every day. When I see something bad happen, I stop and think, and then I say out loud, "This isn't surprising."

33

MY MOM

My mom, Kristina Tindall, would have adventures with me. We would go on her motor scooter and ride it around some parts of the state of Washington. On a sunny day, we would walk, talk, and have fun. We would go to places that were close to our house like the school, restaurants, and the movie theater. She is always by my side on the island and loves me very much. It seems as if my mom knows me more than Dad, and I can see why. Mostly, the reason is that I'm with my mom most of the time and I went to school where she lives.

When I'm at Mom's house, I get to be myself when I'm indoors. It's like no one is there, and no one minds when I'm a little odd. But that's what's cool about being at Mom's house—I get to release the oddness and get it over with. I don't do it anywhere else because then people would think I'm weird.

I learn how to have self-control and change moods in a split second. I'm not bipolar, but it is a useful thing to change my moods. There are easy times, and then there are not so easy times. But mostly, they are easy for me. I learn a lot about manners with Mom, and I think having good manners is a good way to act smart. Well, not act but to be smart in my opinion.

My mom's dad, Harry, was a caring, quiet man. He fought in the Korean War. He really did not like that experience because of the violence and he swore not to join in a war again. It's too bad I didn't get a chance to meet Grandpa Harry; I would like to know a lot about him. He may have been in the war, but he still raised my mom, Kristina, so she became a very caring and loving mom.

With Mom, everything is calm and not complicated. With Dad, it's a different story.

34

MY DAD

My dad left my mom, and he has his own world. I don't blame either of my parents for why they got a divorce; I just let it go. I do almost the same things with my dad that I do with my mom except that Dad doesn't have a motorcycle of any kind. When I'm over at Dad's house, I try to have the best manners possible. Since I don't get to see Dad as much as Mom, I think I should be well-behaved in his house just like I would in any other house besides my mom's.

Jody Allan McNamer, my dad, is what I would call a very balanced person. When he's serious, he's serious to the extreme; when he's fun, he's fun to the extreme. Almost every time I make a mistake, he's hard on me. Mom said that's good because then I will learn my lessons much quicker. Whenever I go back to school in Bainbridge Island from Gig Harbor where he lives now, we will have long conversations about what's going on in each other's lives. Then other times, he will talk on his Bluetooth since he's a busy guy in his business. He's the founder of the company Paraissance Realty. Basically, he's a real estate instructor. He helps people buy and sell houses. He even buys houses, fixes them up, and sells them for a profit. At one time when I was thirteen,

I fixed up a house with my dad and then sold it in Tacoma, Washington.

My seriousness came from my dad and his genes. Since my grandfather, Alfred McNamer, was in the Vietnam War, he was stern and proud like my dad. But unlike Alfred, my dad Jody is more balanced. Sometimes when I see my dad, he has the face of a soldier. I never met my grandpa, but I can sure see how I got my fighting spirit from him and my dad.

My dad once told me that my world was a very sad place. The reason why he said that is because I see the world differently; he catches me saying "I thought" a lot. It's true, I make mistakes like that—like "I thought that was a pipe and not a boat oar for our canoe." But my world isn't sad; often times the plants go down; it just takes rain for them to grow tall again.

I tend to think that my half-brother is more like his mom, and that I'm more like my own dad.

Both my parents are sometimes the same, sometimes different. They are like the Yin and Yang of my life.

35

PERFORMANCE RECORDS

I was five years old when I first performed before an audience. We were singing "Mr. Golden Sun" in preschool. It was fun. And since then, I have had the courage to do other performances. When I was a little older, around six years of age, I did not have the worry of dancing in class when music was playing. I even got a Wilkes Whale for dancing. (Wilkes Whales were awards students received for doing something good at school.)

In fourth grade, our class performed a "famous" play, the musical, *The Adventures of Lewis and Clark*. We all wore costumes made to look like the early nineteenth century. It was a great time for the students of Wilkes Elementary. I was playing Sergeant Nathaniel Hale Pryor, the man who was one of the thirty-three explorers who helped Lewis and Clark during their big adventures. I loved playing that character, and I became very interested in the character before and after the play. Even today, so many of my fellow high school students who went to Wilkes Elementary remember being in that play.

I was in another performance when I was nine years of age. On Bainbridge, we had an intermediate school for fifth and sixth grade called Sakai. When I was in sixth grade, I did the weather every morning for the entire school. I decided to give myself a character, so I came up with Cajun Man. I could not think of another creative character, so I chose that character from the TV show *Saturday Night Live*. I'm a big fan of Adam Sandler and Chris Farley. Chris Farley is my favorite comedian. I always hope one day I can play "The Lunch Lady" and perform that awesome song "Lunch Lady Land."

Almost every morning, I would come up to the table with jeans, a tucked in white T-shirt, and a cowboy hat. I'd say, "Howdy, folks; this is Cajun Man reporting the weather. Today we are having some showers coming down soon enough during lunch break, which is a real bummer because I came with a cowboy hat wanting to herd some cattle. It's going to be very chilly here in the island, so I hope you watchers brought a coat, because it's going to be 34 degrees outside. Woo wee, two degrees above freezing. Not to worry, though; the hot temperature will be waiting to be released when the time has come. Okay, I don't know when the 50 degrees will come, but we are sure it will be today. I'll say it again—50 degrees. Oh, and make sure you hang onto your hats 'cause the wind is going to be blowing during the cold. I'm the Bainbridge Island Cajun Man; thank you for watching." Then it was back to the main anchorman and woman.

My last day being the Cajun Man, I did a special weather report. I said, "Hey, howdy, hey, Cajun fans; I'm the one and only on the island, Cajun Man. Listen up here, folks, 'cause it's going to be very hot at the beginning of summer break, and it looks like a great time to throw your hats up in the air, saying, 'Yee Haw!' to that 83-degree temp. Not so cold for the lowest here today. Only 71 degrees, and I think that must have been this morning 'cause I got a good feeling it's going to be hot all day. No wind according to the computer, so sorry kite fliers, maybe next time. This is all that I have to say about the weather. Since this is my last day, and the crews' last day, I just want to thank you for watching the Sakai morning news. We do our best to encourage you all to do our activities and let you all know what's going on around the school. I know I'm just one of the weather people who tell everyone the weather. But I never wanted to read off a paper. I am saying my goodbyes manually. This has been the Cajun Man from Sakai. I hope you all will have a great summer. Signing off." Then I took off my hat and closed my eyes with a smile at the end and my head tilted down.

After my performance at Sakai, people have been calling me "Cajun Man" every time they see me. It was cool hearing it, at first, but by the time I was a junior in high school, it became bogus. I wanted to be called "Tyler" in real life, not "Cajun Man." I guess people like characters rather than real people. Otherwise, I wish people would know how to ask questions like, "Hey, Cajun Man, what's your real name?" Oh well, people are silly.

Next, I got to act in a play called *The Time Machine*. Everyone thought it was a hard play to perform. I played two roles, the alligator and the guard. The alligator was guarding the time machine while sleeping; the main characters were startled by the alligator, so they sang it back to sleep so they could make it back to the time machine. That was my favorite scene. Not only was I part of it, but I heard people laughing and having a good time seeing that alligator giving everyone the thumbs up. It was fun. I was also playing the guard. The character Max became bad and I was his bodyguard. I did not say much, but I enjoyed that part as well. Even though I was not one of the main characters, I still felt like a star while performing that play at age thirteen.

I already told you about the high school spirit I had during my freshman year. That was no play; it was unexpected, but "legendary" is what people called it. I continued to show my high school spirit during my sophomore, junior, and senior years.

When I was sixteen, I missed the feeling of being on camera. I never thought I would say that about being able to stand up to a wall and perform in a small space. One day, my dad and I painted a green screen! That's right, the wall was all green and had the ability to show different backgrounds covering all the green. I made new friends who have their own video company called: "Must Be Amateur Hour" (MBAH). They happened to be close by where Dad lived so we made a good team with MBAH. I was another character named Big Dog, the retarded boxer. I didn't like the character, even though I invented him, but I did like the videos they made starring Big Dog. I was mostly the guest actor in the company since I wasn't present all the time. But I wasn't always Big Dog. I was also "that other guy who was in the video" person, like an alien (literally an alien in MBAH's favorite series *Star Hunters*). I just hope someday I can have the chance of being a good sidekick character with directors and actors.

At age eighteen, I did a short school play that involved two people. It was called *The Breakfast Special*, starring the customer and the waitress. My partner was sweet, but she played an annoyed waitress and she was great at it. I played the customer, who comes in wanting breakfast exactly the way he wants it. My teacher told me to walk, talk, and think like the character, and I enjoyed being the proud customer who wants things done right. It was so much fun.

I have performed many times over the years. I'm still finding opportunities to perform just for fun. It feels good every time I do it. Maybe, just maybe, I can be a good choreographer, stuntman, and actor in the movies. That would be so cool!

36
NERVOUSNESS AND EMBARRASSMENT

After learning about how I could show high school spirit and that I have the ability to be on camera, it became true that every time I do those things, I always get nervous. Everyone gets nervous when it comes to doing anything really; it's natural for everyone, but before doing things, there is always a reason for doing them. If I do not have a reason for doing stuff, then I do not do it. There are the right reasons and there are the wrong reasons. Climbing up on a roof of Wilkes Elementary School was something I did that was not okay. My reason was to see what it's like to be up on top of the school's roof. But overall, it was not a good reason.

Being nervous is when a person is scared of doing something because something new and unique is happening to that person, like giving out speeches to the class or performing a play in front of an audience. Like I said, it's a natural thing; there is nothing wrong with being nervous about anything.

Having an embarrassing moment is when someone feels that whatever he did was uncalled for or it was something that he didn't mean to do. When people do stuff that they are not suppose to do and they feel bad about it, I call that "having a good conscience," as long as they don't do it again. People can be embarrassed even when they do well. It is very normal to have embarrassing moments, but learning why people do those things *without* showing any signs of embarrassment means that there really is a reason why people do what they do and it shows their effects upon others.

When writing this book, I was so nervous I got a little sick inside. It was a new experience for me, and I was so nervous that my peers wouldn't like me for doing this book. I literally thought that because I'm mostly with adults most of the time. Then, after doing more on this book, I felt very confident for giving this book to my school. In fact, I switched from being nervous to being excited.

The exciting thing about doing something is not knowing what might happen later on. Take for example that you nail the 900 trick on a skateboard on a half-pipe. (The 900 is a famous skateboard trick that allows the skater to spin three and a half times in the air.) Well, you're expecting the amazing reaction of the crowd cheering in excitement! Expecting the positive after every action is a cool way to go, don't you think?

If you have negative expectations when doing something, that will result in embarrassment; then ask yourself: Why could that embarrassment happen? But you don't have to take it from me; I'm just a cool dude wanting to help people understand my world. Although it is true that anyone young and old can inspire so many people.

Feeling nervous is a feeling that says something new is about to go on. Feeling embarrassed, on the other hand, is a feeling you have when you do something you didn't feel like doing in the first place, but you did it anyway. Having that feeling is great because it's all in the good conscience side of things. Combining both of these feelings happens over time. For example, one time I tried to get the crowd roaring, but they didn't show the spirit right away even for a third down, so I just stood with my arms to my sides and smiled. I knew that I was trying to have fun, and people tend not to know what to do. But the class of 2010 was surprised to see a freshman show spirit without being embarrassed about it. Kids, having the ability to have fun is an awesome thing to have. I'm going to be "lame" for a second, but as long as it's the right kind of fun, it's okay. You see, my friends, the way I see it is when you're going to be embarrassed, then it's not really that fun for you. Of course, like I said, you don't have to believe what I say; it's just how I see it.

Knowing these two feelings to me is a great way to know more about any form of leadership. Pretty cool huh? Thank you for reading this chapter.

37

POSSIBILITIES OF CHANGE

When I think of people wanting "change," I think of them wanting to be in politics. That seems to be the common step people view as their hope for change. In my schools, starting with fifth grade, there were lots of kids who wanted to be president or ASB officers or any other role like that. But whenever I see people my age running for anything political, I get very frustrated. Because every time students get elected, nothing ever happens after that. No change, no fun activities, nothing. I mean that's what it is like here on Bainbridge Island; hopefully, it won't stay that way. If there are changes at your school by a student, then nice going, kid; I wish I was at your school to witness that.

Now, many people might think "If that's true, why can't you run for president at your school?" Fair enough; I'll tell you why. It's because, the way I see it, politics is a lot of work with a lot of expectations. There are people who agree and there are people who disagree with choices people make when they are elected. If I were to be president, I would not have time to do anything fun because I would be focused on trying to be elected. I would rather have fun and not work, even though work is part of life like working on this book, but I have fun writing and have fun doing other things. I don't have fun with politics because it's working to have fun for others more than myself. But that is just me.

I sure see a lot of people getting involved in politics, especially kids I've been with since elementary school. I have a good feeling that the more people I'm with throughout the years of school, the more likely they will be running for politics for their schools. I ask myself, "Why do kids choose to be involved in politics for their schools? Out of change, out of impression, or out of attention?" In most cases, it's always going to be for attention. Because nothing ever really happens when the students are elected. Maybe because kids don't have the will to make changes to big things like school. Or maybe there is no need for changes in school.

A couple of times at school, I literally arranged the tables to look like three very long tables and the kids all sat together one time. Another time, I arranged twelve round tables and twelve long tables and formed them up as a giant flower. The kids were surprised and excited about the change. Most of the kids had no idea it was all done by a single student with the help of the custodians.

Sometimes, I've wondered why kids can run for political offices in school. When I was little, I thought it was because the adults were too lazy to make new rules and change a few things. I sort of thought the same thing in high school. Maybe the adults want to see what kids have in mind during their political campaigns. Who knows? There is always a purpose for everything.

When it comes to change, there is the start of a possibility. I'm not interested in "possibilities." All I need are the cold hard facts. Facts are the way to make possibilities possible.

Whenever a change happens, there will be people who like it and people who will not like it. Clearly, there is no such thing as a "perfect change" when it comes to anything for the world. From my perspective, when a change happens, I don't try to change the change; I accept it the way it is. I may not like it, but I can't do anything about it. Ever hear of those protesters who are either for or against war? Personally, I don't choose either side on the "for" or "against" side when it comes to war. Why? Because if I choose either side, what point is it trying to prove for me? I can't protest forever; it is what it is.

World leaders seem to be the "Big Daddy" of all change in the world. There are good leaders and there are bad leaders. Even the worst leaders have some people who think they are/were the best. Same goes for the best; some people think they are/were the worst. There is nothing wrong with opinions because they describe the person's character. But hear this: There is really no such thing as a bad guy or a good guy when they share their characters. People may not like the person then, but at least they know the person's character. No one can change a person's character except the person him- or herself.

By "change," a lot of people mean what they want to happen. Take clothing and hairstyles as another example. They sure become different as the decades go by. People will never all agree and say, "Hey! This '80s hairstyle is for this generation." There's no such thing as a hairstyle for a generation. I wouldn't want there to be because I love the different hair and clothing styles from earlier decades, but it's not possible for everyone to go back and relive those past decades. My point here is that when a change occurs, it can't be done again.

Of course, I'm not talking about changing channels or music or anything like that because everyone would say, "Change it back!" Those things are small changes, but they do not really affect life. Life is bigger. Well, unless music or TV is a major part of someone's life. To me, it's better to experience new stuff and to observe. There are always possibilities for change, but to make change happen for the good, we need to have the facts straight.

38

GROUPS

Being an individual made me think of groups of any kind.

Whether it's in an army, or a "special" group for special needs, or a group for the "cool" guys, groups all seem to interest me.

The way I see "groups" is several people or things combined into one. A group of skateboarders are people who all like skateboarding, or a group of punks all like their own style of clothing and music. It's like what I said about worlds and becoming populations; the same thing is true when it comes to groups. A group helps to determine the population of worlds.

I remember when I was little, my group was the preschool class and then the kindergarten class. It felt like a group, but then I got left out of the group because I was so different from the others. That just made me think about how the "normal" people can be considered a group because they all seem the same and aren't part of the autistic spectrum. Even those who are autistic are not really part of my group because even we can't understand what's going on when it comes to the thoughts in others' mind. In other words, I'm not in any group that represents my trademark except for the routine group which is my family. I'm going to be honest with you; my faithful friends are not part of that routine.

Groups are like soldiers; besides soldiers being in a group at war with weapons, there are similarities. When a big large group of death metal band members and fans are entering an empty stage, they fill the stage with twenty people. When a small jazz club with ten members enters and wants the spot, they aren't going to get the stage because they are too small to take over the stage filled with death metal. Same goes with other groups besides music. It can be the nerd group versus the "popular" group. Or the track group versus the soccer group. Of course, I don't want to start wars, but that's how I see it sometimes when it comes to the number of people in groups.

And then I look at an even bigger group. The biggest group in the world. The group is called...well the earth's population! Yes, we are all in this area called earth and will stay here. We look small when we look at the earth from the moon, but we are all close together when we see it from the moon. Yet in our world, we have separate groups that lead us to war. I wish that we could all just get along, but it's not easy since there are powerful rulers who would do anything to win and not lose. Why can't we all group hug? Yeah, it sounds childish, but why can't we?

A fantastic example of groups is the clapping of the hands. One person claps, the other claps with him, and another, and another until the whole audience claps all together. It just takes one person to get everyone clapping. With groups, it takes one person to form a group.

In conclusion, the bigger the group, the more likely the people in it are to do something. Then again, when I see people protesting something, eventually the police win when it comes to stuff like that. Why? Bigger police groups usually.

39

HEART AND MIND

There is a huge difference between the heart and the mind. To be literal, the heart pumps blood and carries oxygen for the whole body to keep it healthy. The mind or the brain is the most important part of the human body; it controls everything—the lungs, the stomach, and every organ in the body, including the heart.

When I compare the heart and the mind in everyday life, I can really see the differences and similarities between them. A good example is when a boy sees a cute girl in class. The boy's mind and heart both say, "That's a cute girl." But then the mind and heart say it in different ways. For example, the mind says, "That's a cute girl, but I'm not interested in dating her." The heart says the opposite, "That's a cute girl. I think I might ask her on a date one day."

It is true that the mind controls the heart, but both have a different point of view. I never liked the term "Follow your heart" because doing so can lead people to destruction. By destruction, I mean that if young teenagers want to sex it up after following the heart, then it's obvious what will happen in the end. One similarity of the heart and mind is believing in what usually happens as a result. What's the difference between the mind and heart? The mind tells the thought; the heart tells the determi-nation of a person. That's why sometimes when I write notes at school, I remind myself to "Put some heart into my writing." I view this idea as more encouraging than putting some mind into it. I can think of anything and write it with the mind, and I do mean anything. However, I save that stuff in my head and let out everything from the heart when it comes to writing. Once again, I don't follow the heart because that would be boring, and I still want to use the mind as well for everyday stuff. In other words, I don't follow the heart and mind—I use them.

The mind and heart have lots of similarities and differences. If the two are combined, then something wonderful would happen as a result. First, you think about it, and then you put some heart into it.

When people speak, I don't know whether they are talking from the mind or from the heart. When I think of the heart and mind during social situations, I think of the mind saying things to impress people. The heart reveals who the person really is. I've heard my classmates tell their stupid stories about them doing stupid stuff and saying that they enjoyed it. I thought of asking, "Really? You smoke marijuana and you like it?" but then they would repeat the same answer. Who knows whether their answer is coming from the heart or from the mind. People lie just to make themselves look cool. To me, it makes them look ridiculous.

I would like to use a stuntman as another example of how the heart and mind are different. This man hasn't jumped 150 feet in the air before with his dirt bike, but he does it anyway with a large crowd. The stuntman crashes, but then he gets up and waves, making the crowd cheer for him anyway, even though he didn't land the jump. I think the crowd thinks, "At least he tried, and that's a good thing." Yes, that is true and trying new things is good, but when people fail, causing them to break some bones, that is known as failure. Still, people cheer him on anyway for his determination. People "think" they can do things from their minds. That's good, but put some heart into it and the results will improve later on.

In my elementary school and intermediate school days, most of us kids spoke from the heart. We would even say "I love you" without any regrets. We had no fear about socializing that way. In middle and high school, it would take us years to say, "I love you." Surely, it takes a while for the thought to transfer from the mind to the heart to say that. Most of my old elementary school classmates seem to regret or miss those times. I know my past by heart; it's great to remember and to recreate those times. I know that I have to grow up and become a man. But unlike most people, I know how to live in between time. That includes past, present, and future. The mind is a very powerful thing; it gives an extra boost to greatness with the help of the heart.

What I'm trying to say is that I understood what everyone was saying when I was a little boy back in elementary school. In high school, I don't know whom to believe anymore. Everyone went from using the heart to the mind. Hopefully, we will go back to the heart after twenty years.

Sometimes, the truth makes cowards out of people; they always want to hear what they want to hear. Not all people are like that, but I have viewed it in my high school.

There is one thing that I love about the mind itself—it lets me be creative. In my senior year, I made this thing called "The Big Event Club." I'll tell you about that in Chapter 48 so stay tuned.

The heart gives me love for myself and for others. That's how I'm alive.

40

FUTURE THOUGHTS

"My main goal is to finish my book before I leave high school." And that's what has happened. After finishing my book, I wonder what will become of it. This isn't the last chapter, I can tell you that; I just thought that by Chapter 40 I should start talking about the future. My future, that is. There are going to be people who will like my book, and there are going to be people who will hate it. I'm always prepared to know the positive and the negative. Whenever I think of the two things, I become positive for thinking both ways. That's what happened when I wrote those two articles for the high school newspaper.

Just like my childhood, my future is going to be adventurous. There are just endless possibilities waiting for me to experience. I might expect these moments; I might not. For instance, I love going fast. Whether it's on foot with running, on a bike, or on a Jet Ski, it's fun to feel that wind and keep moving. I've always wanted to hop on a gyrocopter and fly all over the northwest. It's been my dream to fly on my own—my comet that will soon be a moon. I was also thinking of getting a car to travel all over the exotic places in the world. That would involve taking my exotic car on a boat and sailing all over the seas. When I was little, I always wanted to travel the whole world, and then I wanted to explore the entire universe. Then I realized that it's not possible to do that, and the earth is big enough to explore...and so is the moon.

I won't get to marriage *yet* because that's just a "normal" thing in this world; people will or won't get married or have kids. Although I do love kids. They make me think of my times as a kid, and I would understand the kids because I once was one.

I feel that college is a way for me to get more money with a better job. I feel like I didn't have enough education from my previous schools. That doesn't mean I can't take college classes; after all, my dad took some before I was born. Maybe I'm hoping to do the same thing once I get done with high school; take some college classes just like what my Dad did. I don't ask for much personally; I'm not a guy who just wants lots of money. Although money is important, I think many people have different talents that are just waiting to be seen by others. For example, my book reflects my talent and my wanting to share how my views are unlike those of anyone else in this world. Only one person can write about me, and that is me.

My future thoughts are that people will read my book and realize there are so many people who can view the world in a whole different way. Each one of us has his or her own unique way of sharing it with everyone.

Whenever I'm alone and outside where it's quiet, I take a long look at the environment surrounding me. I begin thinking how the world outside is how people lived before new technology took over the world. People lived off of nothing. When I think of "nothing," I think of people today who act like they are nothing if they don't have the newer stuff, technology-wise. Remember, nothing is something. I'll be honest, I am one of those people with some technology, but it's good not to have it for a long time and instead enjoy being outside. Putting aside technology, I began thinking how quiet and peaceful it was where I was at, but then outside of that quiet place is the noisy violence that's in the world. When I was about four years old, I used to think violence was just on television and that life was quiet and full of flowers. As I grew older, I came to understand that evil is routine in this world. I can't do anything about it because no one will ever join me to stop the violence. Even when there are a trillion people on my side, violence will never go away; it won't. Rather than focus on the complications of the noisy world, I pay attention to the quiet surroundings and take a nap in that quiet space.

One of my future plans has been to build a new arcade filled with old arcade machines from the '80s and '90s. I like playing video games, especially the old ones. I remember the old games of the '90s from when I was little. They were great, and nothing beats the '90s and the older generations of video games. I would call that place: "Ancient Arcade Archives" (or "Triple A" for short.) No credit cards are needed; no dollars are needed either. (Except for the change machine.) Just quarters.

Thinking about the future also makes me think about Bainbridge Island. I remember when there was nowhere great for any kid to go to after school except Safeway. Since seventh grade, I always wanted to build a bowling alley with a restaurant, a bar, an arcade, a snack bar for the kids, and pool tables. I would call that place "Super Bowling!"

I love the natural fields, but I do sometimes see myself as a "street person." Since I was born in Portland, I think about living in a city. I wander around in the city looking at everything and seeing new stuff I haven't seen yet. A city is like a maze, and I enjoy mazes. Urban life can be simple; that's why I thought a cheap apartment in the streets would be great. When it comes to a city, living rich and living poor seem so equally simple. Except if I were rich, I would live in a higher building and see the whole view of the city with less effort. If I were poor, I would be down below, but I could still see the whole city with experience. It would be similar to how I live at two houses—I have learned how to live with a lot at Dad's house, and I have learned how to live with not so much at Mom's house.

Just for the experience, I always wanted to become a radio broadcaster, or something that involves saying: "This has been a live broadcast event (here in this city). That's it, everyone. I'm Tyler McNamer, and until we meet again, stay terrific." I'd want to do that for the experience of having my voice heard. A couple of times in high school, I would sneak into the football announcement room and play with the microphone. Since there were a lot of people in the field for lunch during the summer season, I would say: "Good afternoon, Bainbridge High School. I'm Tyler McNamer, broadcasting live in your football field. Make sure you enjoy the sun as we listen to the famous Def Leppard." And then I would play Def Leppard over the microphone. I did this until security and the teachers came and told me that they didn't like it, so they told me not to go up there again. I followed their instructions, but then a couple of times, I would sneak in the announcer's room *before* a football game started and say a few things. I would say, "Hey there, all you football fans. It's a fine evening for a good game of pig-ball. Watching from up in the announcing room, I'm yours truly, Tyler McNamer, and in today's game, we have the mighty Spartans of Bainbridge High, taking on the dangerous Poulsbo Vikings. Who among these two teams will walk away victorious? In about ten more minutes, we will soon see. I'm Tyler McNamer, and I'll leave the rest of the announcing to the real announcer. Thank you, and have a great game." Then the announcer came early and kicked me out. I had it coming, but it was still a good thrill to have the self-pleasure to announce games before the games started. I do hope to do more announcing another time, like actually broadcasting a football event or any game event. Maybe in the future.

As I said in Chapter 35, I hope to be an actor, a stuntman, a writer for movies, or even a director for the movies.

I personally would like to do almost everything possible, including visiting every place in the world itself. After that's done, I'll do it all over again.

41

YOUNG IMAGINATION

I tend to think that anything is possible with imagination. Most of the possibilities seem impossible, but they are possible to the human brain. After all, the brain is more powerful than a computer of any kind. I was born with an amazing mind filled with imagination. Everyone is, and I am proud to have mine.

When I was little and would travel on a plane, I would think how maybe planes stopped on clouds to refill their gas and so we can be fed with food from the clouds. That's why when the service people came up the aisle with the food, I would say: "Oh boy! Food from the clouds!" Then I realized that the drinks and water were the same as down below on the earth. I came up with that theory that food came from the clouds. But that's just silly since I was three years old when I thought of that.

When I was in elementary school, I used to think school was like a second house, or a third house when I counted Dad leaving Mom. By third house, I mean that everyone over there treated me like a brother, and I loved the kids over there. But love is such a strong word now that I'm older. Still though, at age six, I felt that the whole world was my family. I don't anymore because family members hurt each other throughout the world. I never thought that the other kids thought the same way, but sometimes, being unique like that was what made me a lovable person. My senior year of high school, I relived my past by becoming the most prideful individual. I was known as "The Legend of Bainbridge Island." I thank those who call me that. Thank you very much. It was an honor to have fun in school showing school spirit and busting out cool dance moves. Usually when it comes to great imagination, the results come in the form of great riches like honor and love.

When I was little, I never really believed in machines and science that makes things. I literally thought that there were tiny people heating up my seat warmer in a car or firing up a stove. But that thought lasted for five minutes when I was two.

I remember when I was a baby, I would drink out of a baby bottle, and I couldn't figure out how the milk stayed inside the bottle even if I tipped it upside down. I was trying to figure out how I could drink out of it if I didn't see an opening. Then when I was a toddler, I figured out that there was a tiny hole in the bottle and I had to suck it to get the milk. I never drank out of a baby bottle when I was a toddler, but it's cool to figure out stuff as a little youngling.

Playing video games is fun. I always loved playing my Nintendo 64. I even thought there was a way to get into the video game world and meet Mario in person. I thought that would be so cool and I had dreams about that as a kid. Then when I was seven, I learned that I couldn't do that, but at least I can pretend to talk to the characters and say, "Gotcha!" and all that stuff. I was a big fan of video games. I still am today, but I limit myself with playing them.

That little story "The Rainbow Seed" I made up when I was little came from a lot of imagination in my little head. I say "little head" because I was little at the time you know.

Another thing I thought of when I was four was that it was possible to fly as long as someone has a cape like Superman. I got upset when I couldn't fly and stayed on the ground, so I saved a toy city instead of a big city.

As a five year old, and as of today, I thought that the same technology can be similarly used in the future, for example the technology used to make the Nintendo 64—same quality but new game. Or older cameras—same quality but for new videos of the future like music or broadcasting. Or even parts of the older cars that can be reborn. I still wonder whether that's possible; then the legacy of that old technology would live on even further.

When I was ten, I viewed college as a place where education is a joke, and it's all about the parties. Education was just a ticket to these parties. I kind of thought about that while I was writing this. Then I thought about my fellow classmates; everyone is going his or her separate way when we graduate. Good thing we have memories; hopefully, people can still remember them by themselves. I'm not sure whether or not I will go to college, but I know that, as I always say, "Drugs and drinking are for cowards." I usually bring down the party house with my own natural instinct. Oh yeah, it's possible. Also when I was ten, I thought that college was the special place to go so you could earn a lot of money after graduation. Then I thought, "What is there to get?" with all that money except for a house and a car and all that living stuff. I thought it would be easier to be a boss and not work for a boss. My dad is a boss, and I can't wait to become one too someday.

Magnetism was so mysterious to me when I was three. I literally thought that plants were metals repelling the magnet from the ground since the earth is one enormous magnet. Especially dandelion seeds, they fly away from the ground. Then I learned that the ground grows but never repels. It's like the earth was made to grow and not push away. I thought of that theory for a while when I was six, and I understood that the world can never repel anything. Everything is in its place naturally.

Imagination is a mysterious thing; no one can escape it. Everyone can learn from it. Whether it's an idea, a dream, a thought, or a view, they all have meanings. Even when it's a "bad idea," it's still a thought. Thinking through something is still an amazing process by the most powerful computer in the universe: The human brain. Imagination is what changed the world and how we see it, and that change all started with the young imagination.

42

ROUTINE

This may sound weird, but I would get bummed whenever school ends. I do get excited that it's summer and about all the fun that awaits me, but then at the same time, I don't have the routine of going to school. Sometimes in summer, I would get up early, still thinking it's time to go to school, only then to remember it's not.

When I was little, I liked to hang my coat on a certain hook. When that hook was taken away, I wouldn't know what to do. I would get upset because that's usually where I would hang my coat. It's a routine thing; eventually, I learned that any hook is a good hook.

Another example of a routine for me is victory. A routine of winning outdoor games in recess. I had to learn the hard way that no one can win all the time.

An eating routine is possible for me if it's vegetables and fruit and maybe chocolate. But a food routine doesn't really count for me.

Ever since Dad moved out, my routine became twisted. It bothered me for years, and often, I couldn't get used to the two different rules in both houses. Mom's house is more relaxing and silly. Dad's house is more serious and busy. Both are great places to be, but sometimes, it takes time for me to get back into the routine for each house.

Even writing this book is like a routine for me; even though writers pause often, still I want to put ideas on paper and then in the computer document.

The routine that I have a hard time with the most is work. School work, homework, yard work, all that stuff. I usually think "Already?" when work is done. School is one thing that I would get used to, so when it's summertime, I wouldn't get used to not working or participating in school. I would get used to seeing the classmates and teachers there and the desks and everything, and then not seeing them for a long time. I'm not saying I hate summer break because everyone loves summer break. I'm not saying I love school because school is hard work, but I do like being in school mostly for the accomplishments I show to everyone. But then I get used to not going to school after a while and enjoy the whole summer.

A routine is not a bad thing; it's a real accomplishment. Then there are some routines that are not that important. Maybe important for me, but after a while, they get old.

43

EUROPE IMAGE

A lot of times I find myself feeling less American and more European. I've always had that image in my head about being European because my ancestors are all from Europe. My great-grandfathers and great-grandmothers came from Sweden, Norway, Ireland, Spain, England, and Germany.

Then again, I speak English and not any other languages. It would be a great gift to speak other languages. Then I could talk to the world and meet new friends, just like I did with that German boy and Turkish girl at school. Later on, I got the chance to know three new girls from different countries. They were from Denmark, Albania, and Thailand; they all spoke English to me and to the whole school.

I'm not saying that I'm not proud to be American, but sometimes I like to give Europe some glory since I have more European in my blood than American. I would look at myself in the mirror and see that I look more European than American. Sometimes, I think my American accent is boring, so I will pretend that I'm German, Swedish, Spanish, Norwegian, Irish, or English. Then again, that can make me look ridiculous since I was born in Portland.

A lot of people are interested in other countries, which is pretty cool. I think everyone can relate to their old ancestors by the countries they were from. To me, this chapter is more of a "write it and get it over with" job because I still think about my other continent of Europe when writing this. I was in Sweden when I was eleven months old. I have yet to see Germany, England, Ireland, Spain, and Norway.

44

SENSITIVITY

Ever since I was a little child, I was sensitive to a whole lot of stuff. Noise was the biggest thing. I was even sensitive to talking; it just irritated me. Even positive feedback was not good for me. It is very weird to think that, but I was just a kid then, and I'm not as sensitive to noise anymore. Although I am like everyone else when I get irritated by a loud thing like a jet plane going by when I'm reading or playing video games. People around me thought I was weird when I would cover up my ears because of a lot of noise, and they were right, I was "acting" weird. I couldn't handle noises; I have always loved quiet and still do. Don't we all love quiet?

What I have learned about being sensitive to positive feedback is that even if I received a lot of negative feedback, it would not make a difference. I would not be affected any differently. But do not get me wrong; I love positive feedback now, and when it comes to negative feedback, I learn how to be calm about it. After all, being calm about it makes me powerful. A lot of times when people say mean things about me, I will chuckle and say, "You don't have self-control over what you say. Go away, you bully!" It feels good to chuckle about it and not remember it again. Next!

When I was a little kid, I never watched the endings of the Disney movies. They always had a lot of scary parts in them. Then when I grew older, I realized some parts are funny. Like Hades in *Hercules*. James Woods is the best! One of my favorite Disney movies of all time is *Monsters, Inc.*. The child isn't afraid of monsters, but the monsters are afraid of the child, and that to me is pretty funny.

I have been thinking back upon my sensitivity to the world and have figured out that it has made it hard for me to trust anyone except for my family. It is true that when I was little, I had a hard time listening to people. I was very sensitive to people and how they talked to me. Even when they were trying to help me, I would reject them. I don't do that anymore with teachers and people who want to help. Often I would test their ability to assist me, but then I learned that when they are there to help, they are there to help.

Mistakes are what I'm sensitive to with other people. Like in a play, I get worried that there might be a mistake. People call me a "perfectionist" when it comes to stuff like that. I always want it to be flawless. Michael Jackson was a perfectionist when it came to his performances. That's what made him great. It's hard *not* to be a perfectionist when it comes to seeing people make mistakes. I still have much to learn about how to relax and enjoy the remaining performances. Of course, nobody's perfect. Michael Jackson wanted certain things in his performances, but they were never perfect. It's strange to think that even when they are "perfect," people are hated by others. Many people don't like "perfect" people.

I was also sensitive about facial expressions. When I was little, I believed that whenever people had happy faces or something that showed that they were joyful, it meant they were fun people. To be honest, those who don't have positive faces scare me. Then after I learned that everyone has different expressions for different things, I began to get quite used to people with unusual faces. It's like positive feedback; not being used to any feedback would make bad feedback not have that much effect on you. The same with faces—bad face, no problem and no harm because every face has meaning.

Even having a routine made me sensitive when I was little. As I grew, I learned that routines change a lot. I don't like it, but it's true.

These sensitivity activities really made me learn how to get used to what's going on that is unexpected.

45

OBSERVING BEHAVIORS

When I was eight, my dad said to me, "Look around your school and see what the kids are doing." At the time, I had a hard time sitting down on my chair during school time. After hearing my dad's advice, I got better at sitting properly in my desk chairs. My parents taught me well in so many things.

Sometimes I take that advice too far when I see other people doing unexpected things. "Do you see anyone else doing that?" I become like Dad when it comes to that stuff. One of my main goals was to be like my parents, both serious and fun. I managed to keep good balance and become a prideful individual.

Throughout life, I observe how people cope with everyday activities. For example, when playing video games online, I hear people talking as if they are bored. I thought that's quite bogus to be like that, so I enjoy my video games and my own excitement every time I beat a level or something. Another great example is when I was at school dances and I saw people dancing dirty. Unfortunately for everyone in the school, I had the courage to write an article about it. Because of that article and my courage, reporters at school became more open with other topics. Observation is always the main key in becoming a great reporter, no matter how dangerous the topic is.

When I look at people who abuse drugs and alcohol and tend to act strange and different, I think to myself: "Hmm...If they use that stuff to act that way, why can't they do the actions without the unnecessary items?" To be honest, when I'm alone, I act crazy and as if I am drunk or high or something like that. After doing those actions, I say to myself: "If they need those items to act like that, they are no match for the natural adrenaline and the natural high. Too bad it's me who figured it all out." Then I thought that other people might have the same thought one of these days. For me, using my own human body to be like the addicts proves that I can be just as or more intense as the addicts.

I look at people who are doing activities like hurdles, snowboarding, and all those really cool moves, and I watch their movements on how to hop over hurdles or turn on a snowboard. It's like having photographic reflexes, seeing things, and trying to mimic them. It's one of the fun parts of observing behaviors. You get to be like others once you know what they are doing. But, of course, not a lot of people like to be mimicked.

When I see people doing something, I wonder whether it's a good thing to do, like rolling down a hill inside a tire. It looks fun, but then again, it will make me sick to do it. Of course, I didn't need to put that in here because it's so obvious; I just like to throw it out there anyway.

Observing behaviors doesn't have to be from another human body's actions; you can observe behaviors in paintings, books, or even movies. Movies, depending on the genre, might make the crew happy and excited if they are making a funny happy movie, or mad and serious when making a serious dramatic movie. Thinking about movies this way is all about thinking outside the box to imagine what the crew might have felt when making the movie. Paintings are also cool to observe because when I look at a surreal painting, I might think about what the artist was thinking when making it; maybe he felt sad or mad or crazy. I love looking at art and studying works to see what they are about. Pieces of writing are another great thing to observe because when I look at Shakespeare and his works, I see that he probably had fun making up new words and trying new things to make the sentences look more fascinating, exciting, and deep. Other authors also create their emotions through their writing, and I think that's cool.

Knowing that I have autism, I took a long time observing the behaviors of the "normal" people in the world and trying to be like them. Unfortunately, it didn't turn out well in the end. Many people think autism is a made up thing and just an excuse for doing bad things. Well, like I said earlier, "Autism is not an excuse." I am flexible enough to say it again for the people who don't agree. What I have observed is that people have different autistic behaviors. I have a high level of autism where I can take care of myself but I still view the world differently. Other autistic people may not speak or may fidget with their bodies. There's a lot of different ways of showing autism. None of them are bad things; they just prove that people are different even when being "normal."

Other than that, observing behaviors is neat because it's like switching eyes with someone else. I know the saying is "being in someone else's shoes" but for me, I prefer "switching eyes with others" to make it more realistic to me. It's pretty neat to be like someone else for a short period of time and then come back to being myself. That's one of the keys to being a multi-themed person.

46

NIGHTTIME

I was inspired by the night sky in the creation of this chapter. Mostly because I see the stars and the moon almost every night.

Sometimes, I would sneak through both my parents' houses just to go outside at night. Both places have different experiences when it comes to the night skies. At Dad's house, there are surrounding trees, so the night sky is shared by the trees and me. At Mom's house, where there are houses surrounding hers in the neighborhood, there are a lot of lights on the roads. It's like there is light on the bottom and darkness on the top.

Nighttime always seems so quiet. It's like almost everything has shut down where I'm from. There are other places where the cities never sleep and everyone is still busy 24/7. In the Northwest, there is always a calm side to everyone. Whenever I see the stars, they remind me of the trillions of people looking down on me—my ancestors, my family members, and my friends, but never my fans. I just self-taught myself into saying that fans love you for what you do but friends love you for who you are. I guess sometimes fans become your friends when they really want to know you very well.

I usually like to dress in dark clothing at night just to blend in with the darkness. Whenever there are other people in the dark, they can't see me, so they think they are alone in the dark and will light up a cigarette or do something else in private. This sort of teaches me what kinds of things people hide when it comes to the night skies. I am never a stalker because stalkers follow a certain person or group of people all the time and try to hide as much as possible, but it almost always ends up being disastrous.

When there is thunder and lightning, another picture forms in my mind of what the thunder and lightning mean. The stars in the sky are people looking down on me, but there are no stars when it comes to thunder and lightning. When there are no good people looking down on me, the thunder is a sign of bad things that will happen to me. That bad thing will cause a shiver down my spine every time I hear the thunder. The lightning is like a warning of that flaw or bad thing before it happens, and it takes off like a flash. I used to be scared of thunder and lightning, but when I go outside and there's thunder and lightning, I try not to cower over a loud noise and a flash of light, because in life, things happen in a flash and affect the spine connected to the mind. It's all right to let it shiver out of the system and move on. I don't believe in theories. I believe in examples that are filled with imagination.

I love the night sky when it comes to a city. It's like a small place where any time is daytime. In night, it seems like it comes alive with all the lights lit up and the cars going through the streets with their lights on. A classy sports car going through the city is pretty cool in my opinion. Or on a non-busy highway, that's pretty cool too. It brings the color of red and white to the road when using the headlights and brake lights. Unlike the lights we have in our cities, the stars will never ever run out of juice to give us light. The sun is a star and it lights and heats up the entire world. Just one massive star causing an effect on the entire world. Super amazing, isn't it?

Sometimes I would dream of being in my own penthouse and looking up at the stars. Then I would play jazz music and relax while drinking cold milk. Milk usually makes me calm and sleepy. Then I would see the full moon and find out I'm still sleeping on my regular bed. Dreaming about the night is pretty cool when dreaming big like that. In another dream I had, I "woke up" in my penthouse and noticed that Seattle was extremely quiet. So I figured that everyone in Seattle must have left for the holidays or something. So then I put on my gym clothes and played techno and trance music. (It's that dancing kind of music you know.) While playing that, I decided to run on top of buildings once again just to explore the city up above and I raced to the Space Needle. Then I climbed up it. Boy, what a view! I saw the water, the city, the stars, and the moon. I knew that this was all a dream and that I would never climb up on top of the Space Needle just to see the view. So I jumped off the Space Needle and landed on the ground, and that was when I woke up. Nighttime turned to daytime.

At nighttime also comes one of my favorite things to see, the aurora borealis. The northern lights shine with the most awesome patterns of light, all thanks to the sun. When I was little, I thought they were walls that just appeared from space. I thought I could never go through them, but now I want to get on a gyrocopter and surround myself in those lights.

But one of the best things about the nighttime is that I get to have a good night sleep. Once I finish writing this chapter, I'm going to bed. Cool, that time is now. Goodnight!

47

MULTI-THEMED MCNAMER

After years and years of observing people, I've learned that I can be either the worst person who is hated by the whole world, or I can be the most beloved man who makes people happy.

I say that because people can be whomever they want to be. A way to see that is by what they do or by what they look like. I view it as their character "theme." All people have themes of themselves that show who they are. By that, anyone can be either the worst person who is hated by the whole world, or the most beloved person who makes others happy.

Small things like barbers or jewelry salesmen have something to give out to the world—jewelry and a nice haircut. They both can be bad jewelry salesmen and barbers by ripping off customers, and by providing poor service or fake diamonds. They can be the worst people who are hated by the whole world, or the most beloved people who make others happy.

I know that is a strong statement, but I view it like that. It's like a level that shows how much people are loved.

In terms of people having themes for their characters, I reject the fact that you can have only one theme for one self. I have decided to be "multi-themed." By multi-themed, I mean that I can be whomever I want to be in different areas. For example, a preschool teacher and a rock 'n' roll guitarist. I have the feeling that people won't agree with the idea of being both a calm teacher and a crazy rock 'n' roll guitarist. To me, that doesn't prove anything because everyone should learn how to control emotions and that infamous natural high known as adrenaline.

I just figured that if I do so much stuff, I would be active and achieve so much stuff. I think I got it from the fact that I have two houses. Different stuff goes on at each house, and it's always busy most of the time. When I get to do anything (appropriately) in the world, I can be a whole lot of themed characters and experience new things every time. I cannot change who I am just because different things happen over time with me, because as long as I stay true to myself, I can still have the ability to go deeper and deeper with experience in my life.

When I look in the mirror again, I can see myself as other people: a golfer, pilot, race car driver, biker, rock star, D.J, street boy, and all kinds of different people. The list goes on and on. I usually say that about lists because I think every individual could come up with a list of every possible thing that the individual can do and make the effort to cause it to happen. In other words, "Take your passion and make it happen" just like in the movie *Flashdance*. However, I figured that the song was saying "passion," which is not a plural word, so I thought "multi-passions" sound good for me. There are so many passions, the list goes on and on.

Multiple themes are what makes an individual colorful in my mind. It's what makes life adventurous. Don't view it as a "Who are you really?" thing. The most obvious thing to say when it comes to that question is "Me." There is nothing simpler than that. After all, there is an "M" in "Me," just like there is an "M" in "Multiple" and an "M" in "McNamer." There is also a "T" in "Theme" and a "T" in "Tyler."

48

THE BIG EVENT!

In high school, we had this ice cream cup called The Big Event. It was an awesome name for an ice cream cup. The name was so cool that it reminds me of another ice cream, except it was a sundae that was somewhere outside the school—I forget the name of the ice cream store, but it has a sundae called "The Hollywood." The store has some really cool names for ice cream. The Big Event comes in two flavors: cookies & cream and chocolate. I fell so desperately in love with the ice cream that I literally made a club out of it! It was The Big Event Super Troops or B.E.S.T. for short. I used "troops" since it's a synonym for "club," and it wouldn't make much sense to call it B.E.S.C. for short. In a way, I created my own homework for this one. To start up a new club, I had to present the idea with a slideshow, write up a speech along with the slideshow presentation, and gather a lot of people to watch my presentation. After that, I went straight into business with this wonderful club. I wrote a speech and read it out loud in front of an audience. It was a long speech. Here it is. The ' mark means that it was what I said along with my presentation slideshow.

Thank you for coming to this presentation. I'm Tyler McNamer, and I have a question for you: Is a man or a wom-

an entitled by the effort of an idea? Good or bad, it's still just an idea. Tonight, I will unleash my idea in hopes of achieving in the record books something that is soon to be remembered for a long time. What I have under this cover is something that might make it into the history of Bainbridge Island. I give to you...the Big Event Malt Cup.

Throughout the entire school year, I wish to make this event a big one. That is why the Big Event will happen to make this year count. It's the Big Event! There is nothing better than figuring out whose time has come. This time has come at last.

'It's time for the greatest game of them all. It's time for the BIG EVENT! The game is on the line; only you and your spoon can save the day. You bring your team together, snap off the lid, and dig down deep in the thick rich chocolate malt ice cream. As the crowd cheers, you sprint through spoonfuls of the best malt ever. SCORE! (Do the dance! Do the dance!)'

I've been eating this delicious ice cream cup for a long time. I love ice cream, and out of all the ice cream cups I've eaten, this one has character in it, especially the message on each cup. For those who might be allergic to anything in this cup, here are the ingredients and a note saying that it's manufactured in a place that also processes tree nuts as well. (In the slideshow, it said: 'Ingredients: Milk fat and nonfat milk solids, buttermilk solids, whey solids, sugar, corn syrup, high fructose corn syrup, malted milk powder (wheat flour and malted barley extracts, lecithin, salt, bicarbonate of soda), cocoa processed with alkali, stabiliser (mono & diglycerides, guar, gum, carob bean gum, carrageenan, polysorbate 80, vitamin A palmitate.') (For the next slide, it said: 'Allergy Information: This product *is manufactured in a facility that also processes peanuts and all types of tree nuts.')*

Now, since this is going to be a club, I'll tell you what it's about. 'This is a fan club for all the people who enjoy the delicious malt cup "The Big Event." This club will have games and a whole lot of ice cream eating. The winner of these games gets to have another malt cup. The loser has to buy the malt cup for the winner. I am hoping to make the "Big Event Stack Tower" (B.E.S.T.) where the cups are stacked really high depending on how many ice creams we have eaten. It will be fun, and delicious.'

A competition is among us, and two opposing forces will collide into battle for the ultimate winner. The stages will be set with team Chocolate and team Cookies & Cream. Now the stages are going to be some places where there is space, and when there is space, there's a competition going on with determination.

It's not fun when people try to ruin the club, but who would ruin something delicious? The games cannot be played using dirty malt cups; they are washed. That way the games are clean. Even when someone knocks down the B.E.S.T. by accident. I'm a patient guy and will restack the whole thing. But it is always important for the destroyer to rebuild it as well.

I've been talking to you about how the club is going to have games; well, I am going to tell you what the games are and how to play them.

Extreme ice cream eating is what I call this game; to make it short, I call it "Ice Head." This game is when two teams have to eat their ice cream the fastest. This challenge will make competitors have freezing heads in the end. Better make sure they pace themselves and not hurt themselves. Unless they have hot heads.' Who will be the Ice Head overall? Only the ice cream cup and the spoon will decide...next to the judge of the game.

Ever notice how the spoons are usually wooden and they break easily? That frustration of getting it snapped inspired me on this next game. Spoon Snapping. 'Two competitors would choose their spoons for this game. This is when they try to snap their wooden spoons with theirs. Whoever has his or her spoon snapped first is the loser.' It's like arm wrestling but with wooden spoons, skill and strength is needed.

I love a good trivia match, don't you? It's a fine way to warm up the brain by knowing a few things. That is why the Trivia Event is created for the club. 'This is a Trivia game with desks and the cups as the buzzer. This is a team match where 4-8 players would answer these questions about the Big Event and sports in Bainbridge High School.' The questions can be anything as long as it's related to the school.

Ping Cup has been a simple game for a long time. For those who are not familiar with Ping Cup, I'll tell you. 'In this game, players would bounce their spoon tops or toss them in one of the ten cups. It's like ping cup, except with a different name and the balls are spoon tops. They do bounce by the way. It just takes skill.' Ping pong balls are the original items to Ping Cup. With wooden spoon tops, most players would be tossing them in, and that's all right with me.

Ever played the game where they have cups and they are mixed well and then you find the cup that has the stuff inside? That game is resurrected here in the Big Event, and it is called

"Find the Chocolate." 'Luck or skill is needed for this one. There are eight cups aligned horizontally. They are all mixed up while the player is blindfolded. The player needs to find the cup that's chocolate. He/she might not know because the cups are covered by regular plastic cups.' Another great classic game added to the list.

When I was younger, I would throw my garbage in the trash can from a distance. Ever do that when you were younger? Show of hands. All right! Who still does that today? Cool. 'All empty cups have to go to the garbage. Not for the Big Event cups; this is just a game. People can shoot their empty cups in the garbage in different distances.' I call it, the Garbage Shoot.

Okay, picture this: 'Ten cups, make two five cup towers, stack it down, and build a tower of ten cups in record time. Along with another Big Event Cup for the winner, another pile goes on the Big Event Tower.' Speed Stack Showdown is the game title here.

Here's a good challenge. 'How far can a Big Event eater eat a cup without breaking the scoop in a certain amount of time? This event will make people upset knowing how the wooden spoons break so easily. Two teams will square off.' People have to dig deep in order to get more of the rich ice cream, and carefully to not break the scoop.

Last but definitely not least, we have a game called Big Target. 'Take turns hitting all the cups stacked up far away. All cups should be knocked down first. The levels go from a basketball to a little baseball. Three strikes or chances are limited for each competitor. Aim well.' It is a different version of knocking down milk jars, but with Big Event cups. Anyone can do this one since the cups are light. Or for a bigger challenge, there might be stuff inside the cups to add weight.

That is the end of the game list. Thank you for learning about them. But we are not done yet. The possibilities are still coming up. Now it's time for me to show you the different contests for the club.

There are game contests, and then there are other contests like art. 'This is when creativity to the Big Event goes to the logo or the icon of the club. Artists of all ages can come and challenge each other on which fan logo is the most iconic. The winner becomes the logo for the Big Event Club. The next contest will return after one month.' Just so that people can get a chance to become the next artist with the coolest logo.

That's right, my dear friends. Fashion. 'Big Event Club fans of all ages can come over to the fashion contest. Dream models will gather to this contest in the club colors. Red, Orange, Yellow, Brown, Dark Brown, and White. These are the main colors for the club. If participants want to be super creative with their clothes, then they are free to do so.' After all, it's always fun to play dress up.

The Big Event Club wouldn't be fully complete without a good Ice Cream Eating contest. 'This may be a long one, but this one is for the people who can eat the most Big Event Malt Cups. No time limit is needed, the most ice cream cups eaten in one day. Just promise me not to get sick. No making up numbers.' And to be sure of that, the people who take this challenge will carry the cups with them and make sure to wash them at room 114 after they are done with one cup.

Next to the art contest, literature would be a great addition to the contest collection. 'A special contest for writers every-

where. They can come up with stories, poems, or songs. So if anyone has a great talent for songwriting or any other kind of literature, he or she is free to enter this contest.' And remember, it takes a while to write something, so these contests are all about taking one's time.

Here's a good one. A dance contest. 'Since the secret message said, "Do the dance! Do the dance!" Participants of all levels can do the dance. There will be music. The dancers have to dance throughout the whole song of choice. In addition, some of the dancing events would require a Big Event Malt Cup on one hand along with the spoon. To make it more interesting, there will be a person who enjoys the ice cream while the other people dance around him or her.' Cool, huh? I bet this one could be a fan favorite for those who love to dance, like me.

This concludes the contests for the club—quite a lot just for an ice cream cup and a wooden spoon. Hang in there; I've got a couple of more slides to show you.

These are ideas on ways to advertise and encourage people to be a part of this wonderful club so that it can be well known, but mostly from eating a malt cup. (In the slideshow, it said: Ways to advertise the club: Video, Walls, Microphone, School Center, Sponsorship, Newspaper, Eating a Malt Cup, Announcements, Posters, Calendars, Sports Stadiums, Morning News, Outdoor Signs, Commercial Ads.)

Now, here's one of the coolest additions to this club: it's called the Special Big Event Area. 'There is a special Big Event area for everyone who wants to eat his or her Big Event without any games or contests. There is nothing but a good time to eat ice cream. Both outside and inside. There will be a sign marking the area. This shows how loyal people are to the deli-cious Big Event Malt Cup.'

If this club becomes so big that there are people who train for the Big Event Club, or for people who love eating the ice cream, there might be a tournament for it. 'Hardcore deter-mined ice cream eaters would gather for the tournament event for all of the nine games. That's nine days of doing the tour-nament. Cash in $2.00 to enter. The host of the tournament (which is me) will pay for the winner of the Big Event Cup. The losers won't have to pay for the winner, but would have a great time participating and getting cheered on by the whole school. Thirty-six people can join. All games are for four people each. Everyone takes turns.'

Or...maybe it doesn't have to be for four people each or for thirty-six contestants; maybe it can be more. These players would gather around for this big tournament event for the ultimate prize given by me to the winner. The ultimate prize could be eating another ice cream, getting a chance to partic-ipate, or even getting honored by the entire school. Because everyone in this school deserves to be well-known and cheered on by others. The moment can be your Big Event, it can be my Big Event, and all together it can be our Big Event.

After the speech...well, actually, I didn't quite present the pre-sentation by copying every word I typed. I learned that it was too long and I had to be a little quick about presenting it to my leadership class. People got really excited about the club and thought it was a good idea.

Time went by. Days turned into months, and not a single malt cup was supporting the club. "What gives?" I thought to myself because I thought the club was a great idea. Turns out that the product "The Big Event" had been sold out! The delivery truck never brought any more Big Event Cups.

After knowing that hard truth, I was extremely frustrated. I had everything planned. Speech, games, activities, fun, ice cream, enthusiasm, and all that. Normally, I never give up when I have goals to achieve, but after I learned about this, I was forced to give up. It was a very hard thing to do. I wanted kids to have fun with a creative club that involves ice cream. Turns out that it was sold out for good...or bad, sold out for bad. Whichever it was, I didn't like it one bit.

It was a huge disappointment, but I did learn something from this experience. I learned how to plan and advertise something and make it into a tiny company just for fun.

This experience proves that expectations lead to disappointments and I needed to prepare for unpleasant facts. Come to think of it, if my plans had worked out, I would have been focusing on that more than this book.

Either way, there are many Big Events out there in the world, all I need to do is "eat" them all.

49

IN MEMORY

"What?! That was a long time ago! Why does it occur to you?" "Tyler McNamer sees that almost every moment counts. I never forget those moments." Those were the words I remembered saying to someone when I was in fifth grade. The memory I was referring to happened in second grade when a boy told me, "I hope I never age. I'm going to be young, energetic, and make good choices. I'm not going to forget you, Tyler. You're my best friend." I find it fascinating that so many people never keep their word; but for me, I keep it in my memory.

One time, we had this week in school that was all about anti-bullying and another week that was about anti-drugs and alcohol. It was my time to test my long lost acquaintances when it came to their memories. After being raised by a Dad who's so into power, I had fun with it. I made up a story saying that a close friend had died because of bullying and another friend had died because of drugs. The response? "Go talk to your teacher; I'm sure she will help you." On the outside, I said "Okay, sure." But on the inside, I was in RAGE! I remember them saying to me in kindergarten: "Tyler, you're my best friend. You helped me, and we should help you. Wilkes buddies for life!" I kept that saying in my memory as a message and wondered what would be the outcome with that message. I've learned that they help each other...but not me anymore. I kept my cool. I just hope someday when this book is published those "kids" will read it and understand. If they don't, I will use my full force of power to get together in a private area and talk about everything everyone forgot.

My memory counts everything. That's why I'm careful about the choices I make throughout life. Yes, I know, I have made bad choices, but I try to forget them. When I think of all the things those kids in school have done for themselves, it makes me think that peer pressure makes people unfocused about a lot of things. In leadership class, people talked among themselves while I made a list of things that the school can do when there's free time for everyone. I've come up with over 100 ideas.

Memories are hard for me; they make me cry because I can't relive them. By the time I graduate high school, it's going to hurt looking back. Man, even I'm crying just writing this part. The cool part about it is that out of all the peers I've come across, I happen to be the one to keep those memories in my mind. I have to be honest with you; a lot of people don't like to cry. With me, it's more of a "need to" kind of thing. Like I said before, I keep and add new things to my world.

Ever since I was little, I've always wanted to keep my character. Even though I can be anyone I want, I always wanted to keep my "good" character inside. The only thing I needed to be sure of...is to do good. Because everything stays in my memory, I must do good. And then after thinking about it for five seconds, I've learned that I'll "accidentally" do bad things and make mistakes in my life.

I've always had this thing with the "kids" in Wilkes Elementary from 1999 through 2005. There have been so many people I've made friends with over the years. There's something about them that got me interested. It's mostly memories that got me thinking. I've been with them, treated them like brothers and sisters, but then I've been left as if we never met before. With that, I came to the conclusion that I should be sworn enemies with them for what they've become. It's a love and hate relationship with those "kids." It does not mean I would spend my life trying to get them to have some common sense because I have much better things to do like eating, playing, writing, and all that stuff. But boy, one of these days once they see my book, I have high hopes of being visible again, even though I've been visible to everyone else in the world. I just wish that when they read this, they will come up to me, asking questions about the past and how I view everything. Maybe even after this book, I could get to know them all more.

Almost everything that happens to me stays with me, and I will never forget it. Just like finishing this book and seeing what becomes of it.

50

I HAVE A NAME

The name's McNamer...Tyler McNamer. I was told that I am gifted and I was born to do incredible things.

After thinking about being told this throughout my life, my response now is...the people who said that are right. No one else in any of my schools has written a book during the course of his or her elementary, middle, or high school years. I am the only one, and I did it against all odds. I still think about a lot of the kids who were in my lower and higher grades in school. It's the people who introduced me by saying, "Hi, Tyler!" to me, and I always say, "Hi" back. Forgive me for I am terrible at remembering names, but I remember the faces of people for something as small as their saying "Hi!" or for something as huge as my teachers, coaches, and family helping me throughout school.

I am Tyler. My mind and heart are the result of my actions. It's why I'm always living. Every day is my birthday because every time I wake up, I feel reborn. I've died countless times when it comes to the mistakes I've made over the years, but I always come back to life all the time.

Billions of people are in the world, perhaps trillions, but only I can view the world in a whole new way that is uniquely my own. Me. I am proud to be one who views the world entirely differently. I never want to be like others because then I would have nothing original to share with the world.

There can only be one Tyler who can view the unique. I am that Tyler. I came up with the view that everyone has his or her world, and that the galaxy is full of worlds. With my world, whenever people land on it, they think they are the first ones on that world. But it takes a short time for them to realize that the world is hard to live in when it is not introduced by the sole survivor of that world. I am he who greets the visitors and shows them through the whole world itself. Often, many of these people are not interested in the rest of the world. Only my true friends and family are the ones who get a chance to see my whole world.

As I see the surroundings of the planet Earth, I notice there are things that change every time. My world adds something new every time, but I never leave anything behind as forgotten. It is a shame that Earth stays the same size because if those things forgotten were all of a sudden to come back now, there would not be enough room for other stuff. The world would then be a crowded place to call home. People do not deserve to get lost in their own individual worlds; if they do, then in real life they will be founding out who they are themselves.

Population: One has been my priority in life, and that priority itself is all about sharing my view with the world. People cannot view the world the same as me, even if they try. There have been countless moments when I feel like I don't need friends in the galaxy because I am extremely unique and different. But then I learned that there are countless people everywhere who want to learn about me just like a child wants to learn more about the tiger species. My name was given to me by my mother and father. It is my name that I will keep always and forever. Allan is my middle name that never rhymes with my first and last name. People remember people who share common interests. I don't relate to any of the "normal" people because of my views of the universe. I don't expect to be remembered as the one who shared the common interests because I am an individual.

My name is Tyler Allen McNamer. What is your name?

A FINAL NOTE

Now it's your turn to take a stand for your true self.

What makes you glad?

What makes you sad?

What makes you mad?

All of these emotions are the main key to finding your true self. Because if people try to be someone they are not, then that is very sad. In my book, I said that I can be whomever I want to be. But I always stay true to myself when it comes to doing good for others and to myself. Remember, "The best kind of freedom is the freedom to do good. It is what makes heroes." When a man or a woman does good to someone or something, he or she becomes a great hero in his or her own world, and soon enough in the galaxy, and soon enough throughout the unknown universe. It takes a single individual to inspire the universe with leadership, determination, ambition, and the way people see things in life. Anyone can be a great hero by doing these things, and everyone does it in different ways. I chose to be a hero by speaking, doing performances, and writing a book. There are a lot of things I can do to prove to myself that I'm a hero. How do you prove yourself to everyone? Drawing? Directing? Dancing? There are lots and lots of ways to prove yourself, but there is only one way that is the way of life. To prove yourself, you have to BE yourself. Because that is the way people want people to be. Not just being yourself, but being TRUE to yourself. Being your true self is how you affect the world with character and color.

To the adults: Take pride in yourself, your friends, and your family. Anyone can make a change into a difference in life when choosing it wisely and effectively so it affects others in a positive way.

To the parents: Your children are truly gifts to the world. They are truly the future of everything when they make wise choices. They can be great people when growing up. All you have to do is teach them and spend time with them. Care for them. Teach your kids how to spend equal time with their friends, their parents, and their family members.

To the kids: *To all the growing girls out there:* You are beautiful. No matter what anyone in the world says, you will always shine. Be strong and brave and show true passion for yourself. *To all of the growing boys out there:* You're the man! Keep it up, dude! Never change who you are. A manly man shows pride, power, courage, and strength. Not strength in the muscles, but strength in the heart and mind. *To all growing genders:* Both genders can be the same when it comes to the inside. A woman can be even stronger than a man. The way I see it, no matter what someone's gender, a person can always be my best friend in that context. Is that the same for you? When it comes to having true strength inside, you can become the most popular group of kids in school. Even to the world! (Wink).

To everyone: This is now the ending of the book. I have shown my true self to everyone. Now it's your turn to show your true selves to everyone. Until we meet again, or until we finally meet for the first time, stay terrific.

ABOUT THE AUTHOR

This book was written from the heart and mind of Tyler Allan McNamer. Many challenges faced him, but he overcame them and went on as a champion, a proud individual. He knew that he was different from all the other kids in school, and he believed no one else in the universe was like him. He was more joyful and serious than other kids. Adults saw him as an "under-aged grown man." Kids saw him as a "special little weirdo." He responded by saying, "I'm not a weirdo, and I'm not special...but I am little." At the time, he was a little smaller than a lot of kids in high school. He was and is a fun boy and loves to have fun, and everyone loves a happy fun kid. What makes Tyler unique is that his leadership toward others and to himself really made an impact on hundreds of kids and teachers in schools from elementary to high school. He even had the ambition to talk to business people one time when learning about how to make this book a great one. He may be a little strange and different, but his intelligence, desire to help people, and even having the ability to write stories and a book at an early age really made him rise to the top. His dream is to be a hero, because at a young age he said that "The best kind of freedom is the freedom to do good. It is what makes heroes." He believes that anyone can be a hero or heroine when that person has the freedom to do good. With that belief, he wrote this book to show you what he meant.